Series / Number 07-046

EVENT HISTORY ANALYSIS

D0731861

Regression for Longitudinal Event Data

PAUL D. ALLISON
University of Pennsylvania

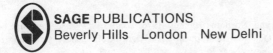

HERB
WESTERFELT

SAGE PUBLICATIONS
Beverly Hills   London   New Delhi

For information address:

SAGE Publications, Inc.
275 South Beverly Drive
Beverly Hills, California 90212

SAGE Publications India Pvt. Ltd.   SAGE Publications Ltd
C-236 Defence Colony   28 Banner Street
New Delhi 110 024, India   London EC1Y 8QE, England

International Standard Book Number 0-8039-2055-5

Library of Congress Catalog Card No. 84-051704

SECOND PRINTING, 1985

When citing a professional paper, please use the proper form. Remember to cite the
correct Sage University Paper series title and include the paper number. One of the
following formats can be adapted (depending on the style manual used):

(1) IVERSEN, GUDMUND R. and NORPOTH, HELMUT (1976) "Analysis of
Variance." Sage University Paper series on Quantitative Applications in the Social
Sciences, 07-001. Beverly Hills and London: Sage Pubns.

OR

(2) Iversen, Gudmund R. and Norpoth, Helmut. 1976. *Analysis of Variance.* Sage
University Paper series on Quantitative Applications in the Social Sciences, series no.
07-001. Beverly Hills and London: Sage Pubns.

CONTENTS

Series Editor's Introduction

This volume introduces social scientists to a new and rapidly developing methodology for the analysis of longitudinal data on the occurrence of events. It is remarkable just how many important phenomena can be thought of as events—divorces, retirements, crimes, strikes, bankruptcies, and wars are only a few examples. Increasingly, researchers are collecting longitudinal data on both events and their possible causes. Unfortunately, ordinary multiple regression is ill suited to the analysis of event history data. As Allison explains, "censoring" and time-varying explanatory variables can produce severe bias and loss of information. Although methods for dealing with these problems effectively have recently become available, most of the literature is difficult for social scientists to use. Many of these procedures were developed by biostatisticians and engineers who have little interest in or knowledge of the substantive concerns of social scientists. Even methods developed by sociologists and economists have failed to reach a wide audience because the presentations have been highly mathematical.

Event History Analysis is the first monograph-length treatment of these methods at an elementary level. It makes a major contribution in unifying and demystifying the very scattered and technical literature on this topic. The underlying theme is that the application and interpretation of these methods is not all that different from ordinary multiple regression analysis. Indeed, anyone with a good practical knowledge of multiple regression should have little difficulty reading this volume.

The emphasis, then, is on regression models. Chapter 1 discusses the problems with ordinary multiple regression. In Chapter 2, Allison shows how discrete-time event history data can be analyzed with logit regression models. Chapter 3 presents parametric regression models, including the exponential, Weibull, and Gompertz models. Chapter 4 explains the extremely popular proportional hazards model, along with its associated estimation technique, partial likelihood. Later chapters show how these basic models can be applied to more complicated data structures.

Given its length, this work is surprisingly comprehensive. It covers nearly all the models that a social scientist is likely to find useful. For each model, there is a discussion of assumptions, estimation methods, and problems that may arise. The major models are amply illustrated with detailed analyses of data on arrests of released prisoners and job changes by biochemists. Allison also gives good advice on choosing among alternative models, and on evaluating the fit of a chosen model.

There is a wealth of practical information on the use of these methods, especially on computational considerations. Throughout the text, relevant computer programs are mentioned and evaluated. Appendix C describes and compares the major features of six different programs for doing event history analysis. Appendix B gives annotated program listings for the empirical examples presented in the main text.

Above all, this volume is exceptionally clear and easy to read. It tells the reader virtually all he or she needs to know to use event history methods effectively, and it does so with a minimum of mathematical notation. It should have a major impact in making these methods both attractive and accessible to social scientists.

—Richard G. Niemi
Series Co-Editor

Acknowledgments

The criticisms and suggestions of the following people led to major improvements in the readability of this monograph: Debby Denno, Lowell Hargens, Jerry Jacobs, Scott Long, Alice Trisdorfer, Neil Weiner, and two anonymous referees. In addition to reading the manuscript, Ron Everett assisted greatly in the analysis of the recidivism data. That analysis was supported, in part, by a grant from the National Institute of Justice. Finally, I want to thank Bruce Turnbull for introducing me to the biostatistical approach to event history analysis.

Acknowledgments

EVENT HISTORY ANALYSIS
Regression for
Longitudinal Event Data

PAUL D. ALLISON
University of Pennsylvania

1. INTRODUCTION

In virtually every area of the social sciences, there is great interest in events and their causes. Criminologists study crimes, arrests, convictions, and incarcerations. Medical sociologists are concerned with hospitalizations, visits to a physician, and psychotic episodes. In the study of work and careers, much attention is given to job changes, promotions, layoffs, and retirements. Political scientists are interested in riots, revolutions, and peaceful changes of government. Demographers focus on births, deaths, marriages, divorces, and migration.

In each of these examples, an event consists of some qualitative change that occurs at a specific point in time. One would not ordinarily use the term "event" to describe a gradual change in some quantitative variable. The change must consist of a relatively sharp disjunction between what precedes and what follows.

Because events are defined in terms of change over time, it is increasingly recognized that the best way to study events and their causes is to collect *event history* data. In its simplest form, an event history is a longitudinal record of when events happened to a sample of individuals or collectivities. For example, a survey might ask respondents to give the dates of their marriages, if any. If the aim is to study the causes of events, the event history should also include data on possible explanatory variables. Some of these variables, such as race, may be constant over time, while others, such as income, may vary.

Although event histories are ideal for studying the causes of events, they typically possess two features—censoring and time-varying explanatory variables—that create major problems for standard statistical procedures such as multiple regression. In fact, the attempt to apply standard methods can lead to severe bias or loss of information. In the last 15 years, however, several innovative approaches have been developed to accommodate these two peculiarities of event history data. Sociologists will be most familiar with the work of Tuma and her colleagues (Tuma, 1976; Tuma and Hannan, 1978; Tuma, Hannan, and Groenveld, 1979), but similar methods have arisen independently in such diverse disciplines as biostatistics and engineering. Hence, there is no single method of event history analysis but rather a collection of related methods that sometimes compete but more often complement one another.

This monograph will survey these methods with an eye to those approaches which are most useful for the kinds of data and questions that are typical in the social sciences. In particular, the focus will be on regression-like methods in which the occurrence of events is causally dependent on one or more explanatory variables. Although much attention will be given to the statistical models that form the basis of event history analysis, consideration will also be given to such practical concerns as data management, cost, and the availability of computer programs. Before turning to these methods, let us first examine the difficulties that arise when more conventional procedures are applied.

Problems in the Analysis of Event Histories

To appreciate the limitations of standard methods when applied to event history data, it is helpful to look at a concrete example. In a study of recidivism reported by Rossi, Berk, and Lenihan (1980), approximately 430 inmates released from Maryland state prisons were followed for one year after their release. The events of interest were arrests; the aim was to determine how the probability of an arrest depended on several explanatory variables.

Although the date of each arrest was known, Rossi et al. simply created a dummy (1,0) variable indicating whether or not an individual was arrested at any time during the 12-month follow-up period. This dummy variable was the dependent variable in a multiple regression with several explanatory variables including age at release, race, education, and prior work experience. While this is a reasonable exploratory method, it is far from ideal. Aside from the well-known problems in the use of ordinary least squares with a dummy dependent variable (Hanushek and Jackson, 1977: Ch. 7), dichotomizing the dependent variable is arbitrary and wastes information. It is arbitrary because there was nothing special about the 12-month dividing line except that the study ended at that point. Using the same data, one might just as well compare those arrested before or after the six-month mark. It wastes information because it ignores the variation on either side of the dividing line. One might suspect, for example, that someone arrested immediately after release had a higher propensity toward criminal activity than someone arrested 11 months later.

To avoid these difficulties, it is tempting to use the length of time from release to first arrest as the dependent variable in a multiple regression. But this strategy poses new problems. First, the value of the dependent variable is unknown or "censored" for persons who were not arrested at all during the one-year period. If the number of censored cases were small, it might be acceptable simply to exclude them. But 74 percent of the cases were censored in this sample, and it has been shown that exclusion of censored cases can produce large biases (Sørensen, 1977; Tuma and Hannan, 1978). An alternative solution might be to assign the maximum length of time observed—in this case one year—as the value of the dependent variable for the censored cases. But this obviously underestimates the true value and, again, substantial bias may result.

Even if none of the observations were censored, one would still face another problem: how to include explanatory variables that change in value over the observation period. In this study, for example, individuals were interviewed monthly during the follow-up year to obtain information on changes in income, marital status, employment status, and the like. Although awkward, it might seem reasonable to include 12 different income measures in the multiple regression, one for each month of follow-up. This might make sense for the person who is not arrested until the twelfth month, but it is surely inappropriate for the person arrested during the first month after release; his income after the first month should be irrelevant to the analysis. Indeed, the person may have been incarcerated during the remainder of the follow-up period so that income becomes a consequence rather than a cause of recidivism. In short, there is simply no satisfactory way of incorporating time-varying explanatory variables in a multiple regression predicting time of an event.

These two problems—censoring and time-varying explanatory variables—are quite typical of event history data. Censoring is the more common difficulty because often the explanatory variables are measured only once. Nevertheless, it is increasingly common to find longitudinal data sets with measurements of many variables at regular intervals. For most kinds of events, such data are essential to get accurate estimates of the effects of variables that change over time.

An Overview of Event History Methods

Event history data are by no means unique to the social sciences, and many of the most sophisticated approaches have been developed in other disciplines. This is a source of great confusion for the novice because similar and sometimes identical ideas are often expressed in quite different ways, typically in substantive contexts that are unfamiliar to social scientists. It is helpful, then, to begin with a brief historical and comparative survey of this rapidly growing body of methods.

From demography we get the earliest, best-known, and still widely used method for analyzing event history data—the life table. It is not a method I shall discuss in this monograph, however, because it is amply treated in standard demography texts (e.g., Pollard et al., 1981) and because it does not involve regression models with explanatory variables. It should be noted, however, that one of the most influential regression methods—Cox's (1972) partial likelihood method—was inspired by the fundamental ideas behind the life table.

While the life table has been in use since the eighteenth century, it was not until the late 1950s and early 1960s that more modern methods for event history analysis were actively pursued. In the biomedical sciences, the substantive problem which called for such methods was the analysis of survival data and, indeed, much of the literature on event history methods goes under the names of survival analysis or lifetime analysis. For example, an experiment may be performed in which laboratory animals are exposed to different doses of some substance thought to be toxic or palliative. The experimenter then observes how long the animals survive under each of the treatment regimens. Thus the "event" is the death of the animal. Censoring occurs because the experiment is usually terminated before all the animals die. Biostatisticians have produced a prodigious amount of literature on the most effective ways to analyze such data (for a bibliography, see Kalbfleisch and Prentice, 1980). These methods have become standard practice in the analysis of data on the survival of cancer patients.

Meanwhile engineers were facing similar problems in analyzing data on the breakdown of machines and electronic components. The methods they developed—which go by the name of "reliability" analysis or "failure time" analysis—are quite similar in spirit but slightly different in orientation from those of the biostatisticians (Nelson, 1982). In recent years, however, these two traditions have effectively merged into a single stream of literature.

Social scientists were largely unaware of these developments, perhaps because the substantive concerns were so far removed from their own. Nevertheless, a vigorous tradition of applying the theory of Markov processes to social science data emerged in the late 1960s and early 1970s (see Singer and Spilerman, 1976). A turning point in this approach came with Tuma's (1976) introduction of explanatory variables into continuous-time Markov models, an innovation that effectively bridged the gap between the sociological approach and what had already been done in biostatistics and engineering. It has taken some time, however, for social scientists to appreciate fully the close connections among these three intellectual streams.

In the remainder of this chapter, I will delineate some of the major dimensions distinguishing different approaches to the analysis of event history data. In some cases, these dimensions effectively differentiate methods developed in sociology, biostatistics, and engineering. Other dimensions cut across the three disciplines. These dimensions serve as the organizing basis for the rest of this monograph.

Distributional versus regression methods. Much of the early work on event history analysis can be described as the study of the distribution of the time until an event or the time between events. This is the main task of life table analysis, for example. Similarly, in applications of Markov processes to social science phenomena, a principal focus has been on the distribution of individuals across different states. More recently, all three disciplinary traditions have focused on regression models in which the occurrence of an event depends on a linear function of explanatory variables. As already noted, we will deal almost exclusively with regression models here.

Repeated versus nonrepeated events. Because the events of greatest interest to biologists are deaths, it is not surprising that biostatistical work has emphasized methods for single, nonrepeatable events. The same has been true of methods for failure time of industrial components. Social scientists, on the other hand, have emphasized the study of events like job changes and marriages which can occur many times over the lifetime of an individual. It might seem natural, then, for this monograph to focus on repeatable events. On the other hand, models for repeatable events tend to be more complicated and also raise a number of difficult statistical questions. Moreover, mastery of the methods for single events is essential for a full understanding of the more complex models. Accordingly, we shall spend a substantial amount of time on the simpler case.

Single versus multiple kinds of events. In many cases, it is expedient to treat all the events in an analysis exactly the same. Thus, a study of job terminations may not distinguish one such termination from another. A life table may treat all deaths alike. In other cases, however, it may be desirable to distinguish different kinds of events. In the study of job terminations, it may be crucial to separate voluntary from involuntary terminations. In a study of the effectiveness of a cancer treatment, it is obviously important to distinguish deaths due to cancer and deaths from other causes. To accommodate different kinds of events, biostatisticians have developed methods for "competing risks" and demographers have developed multiple decrement life tables. The generalizations of Markov models developed by Tuma et al. (1979) also allow for multiple kinds of events. Again, however, the introduction of multiple kinds of events leads to complications that are best postponed until methods for single kinds of events are well understood.

Parametric versus nonparametric methods. Biostatisticians have tended to favor nonparametric methods which make few if any assumptions about the distribution of event times. Engineers and social scientists, on the other hand, have gravitated toward models which assume that the time until an event or the times between events come from very specific distributional families, the most common being the exponential, Weibull, and Gompertz distributions. A major bridge between these two approaches is the proportional hazards model of Cox (1972), which can be described as semiparametric or partially parametric. It is parametric insofar as it specifies a regression model with a specific functional form; it is nonparametric insofar as it does not specify the exact form of the distribution of event times. In this sense, it is roughly analogous to linear models that do not specify any distributional form for the error term.

Discrete versus continuous time. Methods that assume that the time of event occurrence is measured exactly are known as "continuous-time" methods. In practice, time is always measured in discrete units, however small. When these discrete units are very small, it is usually acceptable to treat time as if it were measured on a continuous scale. On the other hand, when the time units are large—months, years, or decades—it is more appropriate to use discrete-time methods (also known as grouped-data methods). While continuous-time methods have predominated in the event history literature of all three disciplines, there is also a sizable body of work devoted to discrete-time methods, especially in biostatistics (Brown, 1975; Prentice and Gloeckler, 1978; Mantel and Hankey, 1978; Holford, 1980; Laird and Olivier, 1981). Because discrete-time methods are particularly easy to understand and implement, they serve as a useful introduction to the basic principles of event history analysis.

2. A DISCRETE-TIME METHOD

This chapter introduces discrete-time methods for unrepeated events of a single kind. While this is among the simplest situations, it involves

TABLE 1
Distribution of Year of Employer Change, 200 Biochemists

Year	Number Changing Employers	Number at Risk	DEP VAR	Estimated Hazard Rate
1	11	200	189 –0 11 – 1	.055
2	25	189	164 –0 25 – 1	.132
3	10	164	154 –0 10 – 11	.061
4	13	154		.084
5	12	141		.085
>5	129			
Total	200	848 – total observations		

many of the fundamental ideas that are central to more complex forms of data. At the same time, the method to be described is eminently practical and can be applied in a great many situations. It can also be generalized to allow for repeated events of different kinds (Allison, 1982).

A Discrete-Time Example

Let us begin with an empirical example. The sample consists of 200 male biochemists who received their doctorates in the late 1950s and early 1960s, and who at some point in their careers were assistant professors in graduate university departments. For a detailed description of the sample, see Long, Allison, and McGinnis (1979). They were observed for a maximum of five years, beginning with the first year of their first positions as assistant professors. The event of interest is the first change of employers to occur after entry into the initial position. Thus, even though we are dealing with what is, in principle, a repeatable event, we define it to be nonrepeatable by restricting our attention to the first employer change. This is an appropriate strategy if one suspects that the process of leaving the first job differs from that of later jobs.

These events are recorded in discrete time since we know only the year in which the employer change occurred, not the exact month and day. In theory it would be desirable to distinguish voluntary and involuntary changes, but that information is unavailable. Hence, we are dealing with events of a single kind. Table 1 shows the number of biochemists who changed employers in each of the five years. Of the 200 cases, 129 did not change employers during the observation period and are therefore considered to be censored.

Our goal is to estimate a "regression" model in which the probability of an employer change in a one-year period depends on five explanatory variables. Two of these variables describe the initial employing institution and are assumed to be constant over time: a measure of the prestige of the employing department (Roose and Andersen, 1970) and a measure of federal funds allocated to the institution for biomedical research.

Three variables describing individual biochemists were measured annually: cumulative number of published articles, number of citations made by other scientists to each individual's life work, and academic rank coded 1 for associate professor and 0 for assistant professor. (Although all the biochemists began the observation period as assistant professors, some were later promoted.) Thus, we have both constant and time-varying explanatory variables.

The Discrete-Time Hazard Rate

We now proceed to the development of the model. A central concept in event history analysis is the *risk set*, which is the set of individuals who are at risk of event occurrence at each point in time. For the sample of biochemists, all 200 are at risk of changing employers during the first year and thus the entire sample constitutes the risk set in that year. Only 11 of them actually did change employers in that year, and these 11 are no longer at risk during the second year. (They may be at risk of a second employer change but we are only considering the first such change.) Hence, at the end of each year the risk set is diminished by the number who experienced events in that year. In Table 1, for example, we see that the number in the risk set declines from 200 in year 1 to 141 in year 5.

The second key concept is the *hazard rate*, sometimes referred to as simply the hazard or the rate. In discrete time, the hazard rate is the probability that an event will occur at a particular time to a particular individual, given that the individual is at risk at that time. In the present example, the hazard is the probability of making a first job change within a particular year for those who have not yet changed jobs. It is important to realize that the hazard is an unobserved variable, yet it controls both the occurrence and the timing of events. As such, it is the fundamental dependent variable in an event history model.

If it is assumed that the hazard rate varies by year but is the same for all individuals in each year, one can easily get estimates of the hazard rate: In each year, divide the number of events by the number of individuals at risk. For example, in the second year, 25 biochemists changed employers out of 189 who were in the risk set. The estimated hazard is then $25/189 = .132$. Estimates for the other years are shown in the last column of Table 1. There does not appear to be any tendency for the hazard of an employer change to increase or decrease with time on the job. Note also that, because the risk set steadily diminishes, it is possible for the hazard rate to increase even when the number who change employers declines. The estimated hazard rate in year 3, for example, is greater than the hazard rate in year 1 even though more persons changed employers in year 1.

A Logit Regression Model

The next step is to specify how the hazard rate depends on explanatory variables. We shall denote the hazard by $P(t)$, the probability that an individual has an event at time t, given that the individual is still at risk of an event at time t. For simplicity, let us suppose that we have just two explanatory variables: x_1 which is constant over time, and $x_2(t)$, which has a different value at each time t. For the biochemistry example, x_1 might be prestige of employing department and $x_2(t)$ might be cumulative number of publications in year t.

As a first approximation, we could write $P(t)$ as a linear function of the explanatory variables:

What wd those values actually be?

$$P(t) = a + b_1x_1 + b_2x_2(t) \qquad [1]$$

for $t = 1, \ldots, 5$. A problem with this specification is that $P(t)$, because it is a probability, cannot be greater than one or less than zero, while the right-hand side of the equation can be any real number. Such a model can yield impossible predictions that create difficulties in both computation and interpretation. This problem can be avoided by taking the logit transformation of $P(t)$:

$$\log(P(t)/(1 - P(t))) = a + b_1x_1 + b_2x_2(t) \qquad [2]$$

As $P(t)$ varies between 0 and 1, the left-hand side of this equation varies between minus and plus infinity. There are other transformations that have this property, but the logit is the most familiar and the most convenient computationally. The coefficients b_1 and b_2 give the change in the logit (log-odds) for each one-unit increase in x_1 and x_2, respectively.

The model is still somewhat restrictive because it implies that the only changes that occur in the hazard over time are those which result directly from changes in x_2, the time-varying explanatory variable. In most cases, there are reasons to suspect that the hazard changes autonomously with time. With job changes, for example, one might expect a long-term decline in the hazard simply because individuals become more invested in a job and, hence, the costs of moving increase. On the other hand, untenured academic jobs might show an increase in the hazard after about six years when many individuals are denied promotion.

With the discrete-time model, one can allow for *any* variation in the hazard by letting the intercept *a* be different at each point in discrete time. Thus we can write

$$\log(P(t)/(1 - P(t))) = a(t) + b_1 x_1 + b_2 x_2(t) \qquad [3]$$

where a(t) refers to five different constants, one for each of the five years that are observed. As we shall see, these constants are estimated by including a set of dummy variables in the specified model.

Estimating the Model

The next problem is to estimate the parameters b_1, b_2, and the five values of a(t). As with the models we shall consider, estimation is best done by maximum likelihood or some closely related procedure. The principle of maximum likelihood is to choose as coefficient estimates those values which maximize the probability of observing what has, in fact, been observed. To accomplish this one must first express the probability of the observed data as a function of the unknown coefficients. Then one needs a computational method to maximize this function. Both of these steps are somewhat difficult mathematically, and neither is crucial to a good working knowledge of how to estimate the model. For further details, the interested reader should consult Allison (1982). Happily, estimation reduces to something that is now familiar to many who work with dichotomous dependent variables.

In practice the procedure amounts to this: For each unit of time that each individual is known to be at risk, a separate observational record is created. In our biochemistry example where individuals are persons and time is measured in years, it is natural to refer to these observations as person-years. Thus biochemists who changed employers in year 1 contribute 1 person-year each. Those who changed employers in year 3 contribute 3 person-years. Censored individuals—those who were still with the same employers in year 5—contribute the maximum of 5 person-years. For the 200 biochemists, there were a total of 848 person-years. From Table 1 it can be seen that this total is just the sum of the number at risk in each of the five years.

For each person-year, the dependent variable is coded 1 if a person changed employers in that year, otherwise it is coded 0. The explanatory variables are assigned the values they took on in each person-year.[1] The final step is to pool the 848 person years into a single sample, and then estimate logit models for a dichotomous dependent variable using the method of maximum likelihood. Programs for maximum likelihood logit analysis are now widely available, for example, in the SAS (SAS Institute, 1983), BMDP (Dixon, 1981), SPSSX (SPSS Inc., 1984), or GLIM (Baker and Nelder, 1978) statistical packages.

Notice how the two problems of censoring and time-varying explanatory variables are solved by this procedure. Individuals whose time to the first job change is censored contribute exactly what is known about them, namely that they did not change jobs in any of the five years in which they were observed. Time-varying explanatory variables are easily included because each year at risk is treated as a distinct observation.

Estimates for the Biochemistry Example

Let us see what happens when this procedure is applied to the biochemistry data. Table 2 reports estimates for Model 1 which does not allow the hazard rate to vary autonomously with time. The coefficient estimates are like unstandardized regression coefficients in that they depend on the metric of each independent variable. For our purposes, it is instructive to focus on the t-statistics for the null hypothesis that each coefficient is zero. (The column labeled OLS t will be discussed later.) These are metric-free and give some indication of the relative importance of the variables.

Three of the variables have a significant impact on the hazard rate for changing employers. Specifically, biochemists with many citations are more likely to change employers, while associate professors and those employed at institutions receiving high levels of funding are less likely to change employers. (These results suggest that most of the job changes are voluntary.) Prestige of department and number of publications seem to make little difference.

Model 2 allows the hazard rate to be different in each of the five years, even when other variables are held constant. This was accomplished by creating a set of four dummy variables, one for each of the first four years of observation. Coefficient estimates and test statistics are shown in Table 2. The coefficient for each dummy variable gives the difference in the logit of changing employers in that year and the logit of changing employers in year 5, holding other variables constant. No clear pattern emerges from these coefficients, although there does appear to be some

TABLE 2
Estimates for Logit Models Predicting the Probability of an Employer Change, 848 Person-Years

Explanatory Variables	Model 1			Model 2		
	b	t	OLS t	b	t	OLS t
Prestige of Department	.045	.21	.22	.056	.26	.25
Funding	−.077	−2.45*	−2.34	−.078	−2.47*	−2.36
Publications	−.021	−.75	−.86	−.023	−.79	−.91
Citations	.0072	2.44*	2.36	.0069	2.33*	2.23
Rank (D)[a]	−1.4	−2.86**	−2.98	−1.6	−3.12**	−3.26
Year 1 (D)				−.96	−2.11*	−2.07
Year 2 (D)				−.025	−.06	.18
Year 3 (D)				−.74	−1.60	−1.54
Year 4 (D)				−.18	−.42	−.38
Constant	4.95			2.35		
Log-likelihood	−230.95			−226.25		

a. (D) indicates dummy variable.
*Significant at .05 level, 2-tailed test.
**Significant at .01 level, 2-tailed test.

tendency for the hazard rate to increase with time. In this example, the introduction of the dummy variables makes little difference in the estimated effects of the other variables, but this will not always be the case.

The Likelihood-Ratio Chi-Square Test

By comparing Models 1 and 2, one can test the null hypothesis that the hazard rate for changing employers does not vary with time, net of other variables. The procedure is very similar to testing for the significance of increments to R^2 resulting from the addition of explanatory variables to a multiple regression equation. The test is applicable whenever one model is a special case of another. This occurs, for example, if one model includes all the variables that are in another model, but also includes additional variables. The test statistic is constructed from a byproduct of maximum likelihood estimation, the maximized value of the log-likelihood function. This is given in Table 2 for each of the two models. To compare the fit of two models, one calculates twice the positive difference between their log-likelihoods. (Instead of the log-likelihood, some computer programs report −2 times the log-likelihood in order to facilitate computation of this statistic.) Under the null hypothesis of no difference, this statistic will have an asymptotic chi-square distribution. The associated degrees of freedom will be the number of constraints that distinguish the two models; in most cases, this will just be the difference between the numbers of variables in the two models. In this example, twice the difference in the log-likelihoods is 9.4. Since Model 1 has four fewer variables than Model 2, there are four degrees of freedom. This chi-square value is just below the critical value for the .05 level of significance. Thus the evidence is marginal that the hazard rate varies autonomously with time.[2]

This procedure for comparing log-likelihoods to test hypotheses about *sets* of variables is quite generally applicable for maximum likelihood estimation. It can therefore be applied to any of the models and estimation procedures to be discussed in later chapters.

Problems with the Discrete-Time Method

In this example, the number of constructed person-years was quite manageable with respect to computation. On the other hand, when a large sample is followed over a long interval divided into small discrete units of time, the resulting number of constructed observations can be impractically large. In the biochemistry example, switching to person-months instead of person-years would produce a working sample of nearly 10,000. One can always solve the problem by aggregating data into larger intervals of time, but that necessarily discards some information. (Note, however, that little information is lost in the biochemistry example because most academic job changes occur at the beginning of the academic year.)

Allison (1982) discusses several ways in which discrete-time methods can be applied to large samples with minimal cost. For example, if all the explanatory variables are categorical (nominal), estimation of the logit model can be done by log-linear methods. It is well-known that with log-linear models the computational cost depends on the number of cells in the contingency table, not the number of observations in the cells.

Another way to reduce the cost of the discrete-time method is to do exploratory analysis using ordinary least squares (OLS) multiple regression on the pooled set of individual time units to estimate the linear probability model in equation 1. OLS is much cheaper because, unlike maximum likelihood logit analysis, it is not an iterative method, and, once the correlation matrix is constructed, alternative models can be estimated at extremely low cost. As an example, OLS regressions were performed on the 848 biochemistry person-years with the dependent variable coded 1 if an employer change occurred and otherwise coded zero. The t-statistics for these regressions are given in Table 2, next to the t-statistics for the logit model. The results are remarkably similar. (For guidance as to when least squares will give a good approximation, see Goodman, 1975.)

Discrete Versus Continuous Time

Before moving on to continuous-time methods, it must be stressed that the discrete-time method described here will virtually always give results that are quite similar to the continuous-time methods described later. In fact, as the time units get smaller and smaller, the discrete-time model of equation 3 converges to the proportional hazards model of Chapter 4. While there is some loss of information that comes from not knowing the exact time of the event, this loss will usually make little difference in the estimated standard errors.

Thus, the choice between discrete- and continuous-time methods should generally be made on the basis of computational cost and convenience. When there are no time-varying explanatory variables, it is usually simpler to do event-history analysis using one of the methods described in the next two chapters. This is largely due to the fact that the continuous-time methods do not require that the observation period for each individual be subdivided into a set of distinct observational units. When there are time-varying explanatory variables, on the other hand, the relative costs and convenience of using continuous-time and discrete-time methods are quite comparable.

3. PARAMETRIC METHODS FOR CONTINUOUS-TIME DATA

Although the discrete-time method just discussed is widely applicable, most event history analysis is done using continuous-time methods. In this chapter we shall examine some of the more popular parametric methods for data in which time is measured precisely These methods are called parametric because every aspect of the model is completely specified, except for the values of certain parameters, which must be estimated. Attention is restricted to situations in which each individual experiences no more than one event and all events are treated alike.

There are many closely related approaches to the analysis of such data, and the novice may be hard pressed to choose among them. We shall try to provide some guidelines for that choice. While a deep understanding of these methods requires knowledge of calculus (including simple ordinary differential equations) and maximum likelihood, it is possible to become an intelligent user with only a modest mathematical background.

The Continuous-Time Hazard Rate

What nearly all these methods share is the notion of the hazard rate as the fundamental dependent variable. In the previous chapter, the discrete-time hazard was defined as the probability that an individual experiences an event at time t, given that the individual was at risk at time t. This definition will not work in continuous time, however, because the probability that an event occurs at *exactly* time t is infinitesimal for every t. Instead, consider the probability that an individual experiences an event in the *interval* from t to t + s, given that the individual was at risk at time t, and denote this probability by P(t, t + s). When s = 1, this is equivalent to the discrete-time hazard defined in Chapter 2. Next we divide this probability by s, the length of the interval, and let s become smaller and smaller until the ratio reaches a limit. This limit is the continuous-time hazard, denoted by h(t). Other common symbols for the hazard rate are $\lambda(t)$ and r(t). Formally,

$$h(t) = \lim_{s \to 0} P(t, t+s)/s \qquad [4]$$

Although it may be helpful to think of this as the instantaneous probability of event occurrence, it is not really a probability because it can be greater than 1. In fact, it has no upper bound. A more accurate interpretation is to say that h(t) is the unobserved rate at which events occur. Specifically, if h(t) is constant over time, say h(t) = 1.25, then 1.25 is the expected number of events in a time interval that is one unit long. Alternatively, 1/h(t) gives the expected length of time until an event occurs, in this case .80 time units. This way of defining the hazard corresponds closely to intuitive notions of risk. For example, if two persons have hazards of .5 and 1.5, it is appropriate to say that the second person's risk of an event is three times greater.

For most applications, it is reasonable to assume that the hazard rate changes as a function of time, either the time since the last event or the age of the individual. For example, available evidence indicates that, at least after age 25, the hazard rate for being arrested declines with age. On the other hand, the hazard for retirement certainly increases with age.

The hazard for death from any cause has a U shape: It is relatively high immediately after birth, declines rapidly in the early years, and then begins to rise again during late middle age.

It is important to realize that the shape of the hazard rate function is one of the key distinguishing features of different models for continuous-time data. In fact, the hazard function h(t) completely determines the probability distribution of the time until an event (or the time between events when events are repeatable). Later in this chapter we shall see how one might go about choosing a shape for the hazard function.

Continuous-Time Regression Models

The next step is to develop models for the dependence of h(t) on time and on the explanatory variables. We shall consider three models—the exponential, the Weibull, and the Gompertz—that differ only in the way that time enters the equation. To keep it simple, let us assume that we have only two explanatory variables, x_1 and x_2, which do not vary over time. An obvious approach would be to let h(t) be a linear function of the explanatory variables. This is awkward, however, because h(t) cannot be less than zero, and there is nothing to prevent a linear function from being less than zero. It is typical, then, to take the natural logarithm of h(t) before setting it equal to a linear function of the explanatory variables. Thus, one of the simplest models is

$$\log h(t) = a + b_1x_1 + b_2x_2 \tag{5}$$

where a, b_1, and b_2 are constants to be estimated. In this equation h(t) is a function of the explanatory variables, but it does not depend on time. A hazard that is constant over time implies an exponential distribution for the time until event occurrence and, hence, this is often referred to as the exponential regression model.

Specifying a constant hazard is usually unrealistic, however. If the event is a death, for example, the hazard should increase with time, due to aging of the organism. On the other hand, if the event is an employer change, the hazard is likely to decline with time as the individual becomes more invested in the job. We can relax the assumption of a constant hazard by allowing the log of the hazard to increase or decrease linearly with time, i.e.,

$$\log h(t) = a + b_1x_1 + b_2x_2 + ct \tag{6}$$

25

where c is a constant which may be either positive or negative. Because this model gives rise to a Gompertz distribution for the time until event occurrence, it is convenient to refer to equation 6 as the Gompertz regression model.

Alternatively, let us consider a model in which the log of the hazard increases or decreases linearly with the log of time:

$$\text{Weibull} \quad \log h(t) = a + b_1 x_1 + b_2 x_2 + c \log t \qquad [7]$$

where c is constrained to be greater than -1. This model generates a Weibull distribution for the time until event occurrence. Hence, it is often referred to as a Weibull regression model.

There are many other models that differ only in the way that time enters the equation, but these three are the most common. For additional information on these three models, see Lawless (1982). Although time appears to be just another explanatory variable in the Weibull and Gompertz models, its role is much more fundamental. In particular, the difference between equations 6 and 7 requires an entirely different estimation procedure rather than a simple transformation from time to log time. *Why? + What?*

Note that neither the Weibull model nor the Gompertz model allows for a U shape or an inverted U shape; the hazard may either decrease or increase with time, but may not change direction. This is a disadvantage in some applications. Later we shall consider some models that do not have this restriction.

Notice also that none of these models has a random disturbance term. They are not deterministic models, however, because there is random variation in the relationship between the unobservable dependent variable h(t) and the observed length of the time interval. Still, there are some who argue that these models should include a disturbance term, an issue that will be discussed at the end of this chapter.

Maximum Likelihood Estimation

Writing down models is easy. The difficulty comes in trying to estimate them, especially with censored data. In the late 1960s, statisticians developed maximum likelihood procedures for the exponential regression model (Zippin and Armitage, 1966; Glasser, 1967), and it was not long before maximum likelihood was available for many other models as well. Appendix A discusses maximum likelihood estimation of parametric models in some detail, but it is worth mentioning some of the general properties here.

As an estimation method for censored data, maximum likelihood is hard to beat. It combines the censored and uncensored observations in such a way as to produce estimates that are asymptotically unbiased, normally distributed and efficient (i.e., have minimum sampling variance). Unfortunately, "asymptotically" means that these properties are only approximations that improve as the sample gets larger. No one knows how well they hold in small samples or how large is large enough. In the absence of compelling alternative methods, however, maximum likelihood is widely used with both small and large samples.

There are many computer programs available to do maximum likelihood estimation of one or more of these models. The RATE program (Tuma, 1979) will estimate the exponential model, the Gompertz model, and several extensions of the Gompertz model. The GLIM program (Baker and Nelder, 1978) will estimate the exponential and Weibull regression models (in version 3), but only by employing special procedures that are not documented in the manual (Aitkin and Clayton, 1980; Roger and Peacock, 1983). Weibull and exponential models can also be estimated with two author-distributed programs, CENSOR (Meeker and Duke, 1981) and SURVREG (Preston and Clarkson, 1983).

An Empirical Example

To illustrate these methods, we shall apply the exponential regression model to the criminal recidivism data (Rossi et al., 1980) that were briefly described in Chapter 1. The sample consisted of 432 males who were followed for one year after their release from Maryland state prisons. The study was actually a randomized field experiment in which approximately half the men received financial assistance while the other half served as a control group. During the follow-up year, the subjects were interviewed monthly regarding their experiences during the previous month. At the end of the year, a search was made through district court records for data on arrests and convictions.

The event of interest is the first arrest after release, and the aim is to determine how the hazard for an arrest depends on the following explanatory variables: age, race, years of schooling, marital status, age at earliest known arrest, number of previous theft arrests, parole status, financial assistance, prior work experience, and number of weeks employed during the first three months after release. With the exception of the last variable, all of these variables are clearly constant in value over the follow-up period. While employment status is obviously change-

TABLE 3
Coefficient Estimates for Three Models of Recidivism

| | 1 | | 2 | | 3 | |
| | Exponential | | Proportional Hazards | | Time-Dependent Proportional Hazards | |
Explanatory Variables	b	t	b	t	b	t
Financial aid (D)[a]	−.325	−1.69	−.337	−1.76	−.333	−1.74
Age at release	−.067	−2.89**	−.069	−2.94**	−.064	−2.78**
Black (D)	.280	.90	.286	.92	.354	1.13
Work experience (D)	−.117	−.53	−.122	−.55	−.012	−.06
Married (D)	−.414	−1.08	−.426	−1.11	−.334	−.87
Paroled (D)	−.037	−.19	−.035	−.18	−.075	−.38
Prior arrests	.095	3.21**	.101	3.36**	.100	3.31**
Age at earliest arrest	.070	2.30*	.071	2.35*	.077	2.48*
Education	−.263	−1.96*	−.264	−1.96*	−.293	−2.12*
Weeks worked	−.039	−1.76	−.039	−1.78	–	–
Worked (D)	–	–	–	–	−1.397	−5.65**
Constant	−3.860		–		–	

a. (D) indicates dummy variable.
*Significant at .05 level.
**Significant at .01 level.

able over the full year after release, this analysis will treat it as constant over time. Later, we shall examine a model allowing employment status to vary over time.

Most programs for estimating event history models require that the data on the dependent variable be input in two parts: a dummy variable indicating whether or not the event (in this case an arrest) occurred during the observation period, and a variable giving either the time of the event (if it occurred) or the time of censoring. In this example, time was measured in weeks since release. Thus, for those who were arrested, the second component of the dependent variable was the number of weeks from release to arrest. For those who were not arrested, the week number was 52, the last week that they were observed. Estimates for an exponential regression model were obtained with the GLIM program (see Appendix B for program listing), and are reported in panel 1 of Table 3.

Interpreting the coefficient estimates is much like interpreting unstandardized regression coefficients. For example, the coefficient of −.067 for age at release means that each additional year of life reduces the log of the hazard by .067, controlling for other variables. A some-

28

what more intuitive interpretation is obtained by exponentiating the coefficients (taking their antilogs). That is, if b is the coefficient, compute exp(b), which means raising the number e (approximately 2.718) to the b power. The interpretation is then as follows: For each unit increase in an explanatory variable, the hazard is multiplied by its exponentiated coefficient. Further, computing $100(\exp(b) - 1)$ gives the percentage change in the hazard with each one unit change in the explanatory variable. For example, the coefficient for number of prior arrests is .095, and exp(.095) = 1.10. This tells us that each additional prior arrest increases the hazard by an estimated 10 percent. For dummy variables, the exponentiated coefficient gives the relative hazard for the groups corresponding to values of the dummy variable, again controlling for other variables. The coefficient for the dummy variable for financial aid, for instance, is −.325, which gives exp(−.325) = .72. This means that the hazard of arrest for those who received financial aid was about 72 percent of the hazard for those who did not recieve aid. Alternatively, since 1 / .72 = 1.38, we can say that the hazard for those who did not receive aid was about 38 percent larger than the hazard for those who did receive aid.

The ratios of the estimates to their standard errors are also useful statistics. For moderate to large samples, these can be treated like t-statistics in an ordinary multiple regression. Thus if the ratio exceeds 2, the coefficient is significantly different from zero at the .05 level with a two-tailed test. Also the relative sizes of these ratios can be used to gauge the relative importance of the variables. In this example, we see that only four of the 10 variables have effects which are definitely significant: age at release, age at earliest known arrest, education, and number of prior arrests. The effect of financial aid is significant with a one-tailed test but not with a two-tailed test. With the exception of age at first arrest, all these effects are in the expected direction. Thus, the positive sign of prior arrests means that those with many prior arrests have a higher risk of being arrested at any point in time.[3]

Censoring

In both this example and the biochemistry example in Chapter 2, censoring occurred at the same point in time for all individuals. Thus, any released inmates who had still not been arrested at the end of 12 months were considered censored. This is sometimes called fixed censoring or Type I censoring. Under fixed censoring, it is unnecessary to make any further assumptions about the nature of the censoring process.

In many situations, however, the censoring times will vary across individuals. This occurs when individuals drop out of the study, for one reason or another, before the end of the observation period. Possible reasons include death, migration out of the population at risk, failure to locate the individual in later interviews, or refusal to continue in the study. When censoring times vary across individuals (and are not under the control of the investigator) censoring is said to be random. Random censoring also includes designs in which observation *ends* at the same time for all individuals, but begins at different times.

When censoring is random, virtually all event history methods assume that the censoring times are independent of the times at which events occur, controlling for the explanatory variables in the regression model. This assumption would be violated, for example, if individuals who were more likely to be arrested were also more likely to migrate out of the study area. Although it is possible to develop models which allow for dependence between censoring and the occurrence of the event of interest, this is rarely done. The main reason why it is not often done (aside from the inconvenience of a nonstandard model) is that it is impossible to test whether any dependence model is more appropriate than the independence model (Tsiatis, 1975). In other words, the data can never tell you which is the correct model.

It is possible, however, to get some idea of how sensitive one's analysis is to violations of the independence assumption. In essence, the sensitivity analysis consists of reestimating the model twice, each time treating the censored observations in a different extreme way. The first step is to redo the analysis with the data altered so that censored observations experience an event at the time of censoring. In most cases, this is easily accomplished by recoding the dummy variable which indicates whether or not an observation is censored so that all observations have a value of 1. The second step is to redo the analysis so that the censoring times are all equal to the longest time observed in the sample, regardless of whether that time is censored or uncensored. Thus, even if some of the released prisoners had been censored before the end of the one-year period, their censoring times would be set to one year. If the parameter estimates resulting from the standard analysis are similar to those obtained from these two extreme situations, one can be confident that violations of the independence assumption are unimportant (Peterson, 1976). Note that this approach to censoring can be used with any of the methods discussed in later chapters.

Some Other Models

The three models considered above—the exponential, the Weibull, and the Gompertz—are all members of a general class of models known as proportional hazards models. In the next chapter, we shall see how to estimate this general class without having to choose a particular member. Before leaving the subject of parametric models, however, let us briefly consider another general class of models known either as accelerated failure time models (Kalbfleisch and Prentice, 1980) or as location-scale models (Lawless, 1982). If T is the elapsed time until an event occurs, this class can be written as

$$\log T = a + b_1 x_1 + b_2 x_2 + \ldots + u \qquad [8]$$

where u is a random disturbance term that is independent of the x's.

Different members of this class have different distributions for the disturbance term u. Distributions that are commonly assumed include the normal, log-gamma, logistic, and extreme value distributions. These give rise, respectively, to log-normal, gamma, log-logistic, and Weibull distributions for T. Thus, the Weibull regression model is a member of both the proportional hazards class and the accelerated failure time class. In fact, it can be shown that the Weibull (and its special case—the exponential) is the only model that falls into both of these classes.

The accelerated failure time models can be reexpressed so that the dependent variable is the hazard rate rather than log T, but these expressions tend to be quite complicated. The lognormal and log-logistic models are unusual in that the hazard is a nonmonotonic function of time; it first increases, reaches a peak, and then gradually declines with time. When there is no censoring of T, the accelerated failure time models can be consistently estimated by ordinary least squares regression of log T on the explanatory variables. In the presence of censoring, however, one must usually resort to maximum likelihood estimation. For details see Lawless (1982).

Choosing a Model

How does one choose among alternative parametric models? As with most statistical methods, it is rather difficult to codify the procedures involved in choice of a model. There are many factors that should legitimately enter the decision and none can be easily quantified. Invariably there is tension among mathematical convenience, theoretical appropriateness, and empirical evidence.

With models of the sort we have just been discussing, the key differentiating factor is the way in which the hazard rate depends on time. The first choice is between the exponential regression model, in which there is no dependence on time, and all other models. From a mathematical and computational point of view, the exponential model is very attractive. For this reason, it is often useful as a first approximation even when it is known to be false. Substantive theory, on the other hand, will usually suggest many reasons why the hazard should change with time. As for empirical evidence, there are well-known graphical methods for assessing whether event times have an exponential distribution (Gross and Clark, 1975; Elandt-Johnson and Johnson, 1980, Ch. 7; Lawless, 1982, Ch. 2). These can be quite useful if the explanatory variables have relatively weak effects on the hazard. If effects are strong, however, the graphical methods may show a declining hazard even when the true hazard is constant over time.

A better approach is to fit the exponential regression model with explanatory variables and then examine its fit to the data. This can be done by using the residual plots described by Lawless (1982) for evidence of departure from exponentiality. A more formal method for testing the fit of the exponential regression model derives from the fact that the exponential is a special case of several of the models considered thus far, including the Weibull, Gompertz, and gamma regression models. The procedure is to fit both the exponential and one of these other models by maximum likelihood. The relative fit of the two models can then be tested by comparing log-likelihoods as described in Chapter 2. Rejection of the exponential model is indicated when its log-likelihood differs significantly from that of the alternative model.

If the exponential model is rejected, one must then choose between monotonic models (in which the hazard always increases or always decreases with time) and nonmonotonic models (in which the hazard may sometimes increase and sometimes decrease). Again, both substantive theory and the graphical methods referenced above can be helpful in making this choice. As before, however, one must be wary of univariate graphs for assessing the shape of the hazard function. Strong effects of explanatory variables can make the evidence misleading. As an alternative to univariate graphical techniques, residual plots are available for assessing the fit of a chosen model (Lawless, 1982).

As noted above, the lognormal and log-logistic models have nonmonotonic hazard functions in which the hazard first increases and then decreases. This might be appropriate for many kinds of social mobility in which there is (a) an initial "resting period" after the previous move, (b) an increase in the risk of a move as the resting period is completed, and (c) a decline in the risk of a move as individuals become more invested in a particular social location. On the other hand, there is no convenient parametric model to represent U-shaped hazard functions. If there is strong departure from monotonicity, it is often better to shift to the semiparametric, proportional hazards model discussed in the next chapter.

Within the class of monotonic models, choice of model will often be based on mathematical and computational convenience. Social theory and empirical evidence are typically inadequate to discriminate between, say, a Weibull model and a Gompertz model.[4]

Unobserved Sources of Heterogeneity

Many social theories imply or suggest that the hazard rate for some event should be increasing or decreasing with time. For example, certain job search theories imply that the hazard rate for obtaining a job should increase with the length of unemployment (Heckman and Singer, 1982). While the procedures described in the preceding section on model choice can be useful in testing such hypotheses, great caution is required in trying to draw inferences about the effect of time on the hazard rate. The basic problem was mentioned above, but is worth some elaboration here. Even if the hazard rate is constant over time for each individual, differences (across individuals) in the hazard rate that are not incorporated into the model will tend to produce evidence for a *declining* hazard rate (Heckman and Singer, 1982).

Intuitively, what happens is that individuals with high hazard rates experience events early and are then eliminated from the risk set. As time goes on, this selection process yields risk sets that contain individuals with predominantly low risks. The upshot is that it is extremely difficult to distinguish hazard rates that are truly declining with time from simple variation in hazard rates across individuals. On the other hand, if one observes evidence for an *increasing* hazard rate, this can always be regarded as evidence that the hazard really increases with time.

A simple way to deal with the problem of heterogeneity is to explicitly incorporate the sources of that heterogeneity as explanatory variables in the model. But it would be unrealistic to assume that all such sources of heterogeneity can be measured and included. This problem has been a matter of concern for sociologists and econometricians working with these models, and there have been attempts to expand the model to include a disturbance term representing the unobserved sources of heterogeneity. In particular, Heckman and Singer (1982) have considered an extended Weibull model,

$$\log h(t) = a + b_1 x_1 + b_2 x_2 + c \log t + u \qquad [9]$$

where u is a random disturbance. In principle, estimation of such a model should allow one to separate the effects of time from the unobserved heterogeneity. In practice, they have found that estimates of c and the b coefficients are highly sensitive to the choice of a particular distribution for u. Although work is being done to remedy this problem, it is still too early to conclude whether the approach will be generally useful.

Biostatisticians have been remarkably unconcerned about the problem of unmeasured sources of heterogeneity, though there is every reason to suspect that it will be just as serious for biological as for social phenomena. Their attitude seems to be that the consequence of such heterogeneity will be mainly to change the shape of the distribution of T (the time of the event), and that this can be accommodated by specifying a different distribution for T (e.g., a Gompertz instead of a Weibull), or by using a more general model (e.g., the proportional hazards model considered in the next chapter). This position is reasonable so long as one is primarily concerned with estimating the effects of the explanatory variables and is not particularly interested in testing hypotheses about the effect of time.

4. PROPORTIONAL HAZARDS AND PARTIAL LIKELIHOOD

The methods discussed and applied in Chapter 3 represent a tremendous advance over ad hoc approaches to event history data, but they still have some disadvantages. First, it is necessary to decide how the hazard rate depends on time, and there may be little information on which to base such a choice. Moreover, if the hazard function is believed to be nonmonotonic, it may be difficult to find a model with the appropriate shape. Much experience with these models suggests that the coefficient estimates are not terribly sensitive to the choice of the hazard function, but one can never be sure what will happen in any particular situation. The second, and perhaps the more serious, problem is that these models do not allow for explanatory variables whose values change over time. While it is possible to develop fully parametric models that include time-varying explanatory variables (Tuma, 1979; Flinn and Heckman, 1982a, 1982b) estimation of these models is somewhat cumbersome.

Both these problems were solved in 1972 when David Cox, a British statistician, published a paper entitled "Regression Analysis and Life

34

Tables," in which he proposed a model and an estimation method that have since become extremely popular, especially in biomedical research.

The Proportional Hazards Model

Commonly referred to as the "proportional hazards model," Cox's model is a simple generalization of the parametric models we have just considered. We shall postpone, for the moment, a consideration of models with time-varying explanatory variables. For two time-constant variables, the model may be written as

$$\log h(t) = a(t) + b_1 x_1 + b_2 x_2 \qquad [10]$$

where $a(t)$ can be any function of time. Because this function does not have to be specified, the model is often described as partially parametric or semiparametric. It is called the proportional hazards model because for any two individuals at any point in time, the ratio of their hazards is a constant. Formally, for any time t, $h_i(t)/h_j(t) = c$ where i and j refer to distinct individuals and c may depend on explanatory variables but not on time. Despite the name, this is not a crucial feature of Cox's model because the hazards cease to be proportional as soon as one introduces time-varying explanatory variables.

Partial Likelihood

Again, it is easy to write down such models but difficult to devise ways to estimate them. Cox's most important contribution was to propose a method called partial likelihood which bears many similarities to ordinary maximum likelihood estimation. Mathematical details on partial likelihood are given in Appendix A, but some general properties can be mentioned here. The method relies on the fact that the likelihood function for data arising from the proportional hazards model can be factored into two parts: One factor contains information only about the coefficients b_1 and b_2; the other factor contains information about b_1, b_2, and the function $a(t)$. Partial likelihood simply discards the second factor and treats the first factor as though it were an ordinary likelihood function. This first factor depends only on the *order* in which events occur, not on the exact times of occurrence.[5]

The resulting estimators are asymptotically unbiased and normally distributed. They are not fully efficient because some information is lost by ignoring the exact times of event occurrence. But the loss of efficiency is usually so small that it is not worth worrying about (Efron, 1977).

It is difficult to exaggerate the impact of Cox's work on the practical analysis of event history data. In recent years, his 1972 paper has been cited well over 100 times a year in the world scientific literature. In the judgment of many, it is unequivocally the best all-around method for estimating regression models with continuous-time data.

Other methods may be more appropriate in cases where a major substantive concern is with the dependence of the hazard on time. For example, the principle of cumulative inertia suggests that the longer an individual is in a particular state, the less likely he is to leave that state (McGinnis, 1968). Such a hypothesis could not be tested under partial likelihood estimation. In most cases, however, the main concern is with the effects of the explanatory variables, and the dependence on time is of little interest. As noted in Chapter 3, moreover, testing hypotheses about the effect of time on the hazard is difficult under any model because unmeasured sources of heterogeneity usually contaminate that effect.

Computer programs for partial likelihood estimation for the proportional hazards model are now widely available as part of the SAS (SAS Institute, 1983) and BMDP (Dixon, 1981) statistical packages. Other publicly available programs to do partial likelihood are RATE (Tuma, 1979) and SURVREG (Preston and Clarkson, 1983). The SAS supplementary procedure PHGLM is very easy to use but does not allow for time-varying explanatory variables. Neither does the proportional hazards model in RATE.

Partial Likelihood Applied
to an Empirical Example

Let us return to the criminal recidivism data of Rossi et al. (1980) to see what happens when a proportional hazards model is estimated. Using the same explanatory variables as for the exponential regression model, estimates were obtained using the SAS procedure PHGLM. (A program listing is given in Appendix B.) Results are reported in panel 2 of Table 3. Both the coefficient estimates and the ratios of the estimates to their standard errors (t-statistics) are almost identical to those produced by the exponential regression model. This should not be too surprising since the exponential model is just a proportional hazards model in which the arbitrary function a(t) is fixed at a constant value. The fact that the estimates are so similar suggests that the hazard for an arrest does not change much over the 12-month period. Given these results, there would be no point in estimating a Weibull regression model; since the Weibull model falls between the exponential and proportional hazards models in generality, the estimates would hardly vary from those in panels 1 and 2 of Table 3.

Time-Varying Explanatory Variables

The proportional hazards model can be extended easily to allow for explanatory variables that change in value over time. A model with two explanatory variables, one constant and one varying over time, may be written as

$$\log h(t) = a(t) + b_1 x_1 + b_1 x_2(t) \qquad [11]$$

where, as before, $a(t)$ may be any function of time. This model says that the hazard at time t depends on the value of x_2 at the same time t. In some cases, however, there may be reason to believe that there is a lag between a change in a variable and the effect of that change on the hazard. For example, if one is interested in the effect of a bout of unemployment on the hazard of divorce, it might be plausible to suspect that there is a lag between the loss of a job and an increase in the hazard. If the suspected lag is two months (and time is measured in months) the model can be modified to read

$$\log h(t) = a(t) + b_1 x_1 + b_2 x_2(t - 2) \qquad [12]$$

With or without lags, models with time-varying explanatory variables can be estimated using the partial likelihood method described earlier. The derivation of the partial likelihood function is essentially the same with time-varying explanatory variables, but the computer algorithms for constructing and maximizing that likelihood function are more complex. Hence, not all programs for partial likelihood estimation will handle time-varying explanatory variables (sometimes referred to as "time-dependent covariates").

Returning to the recidivism example, we noted earlier that the variable "weeks employed during the first three months after release" is merely a substitute for what is actually a time-varying explanatory variable. What one would ideally like to know is how the hazard is affected by employment status at any given point in time during the one-year follow-up. This question can be answered because the data set includes information on whether the individual was employed during each of the 52 weeks of observation. Using BMDP2L, a proportional hazards model was estimated that included a dummy variable for employment status as a time-varying explanatory variable. (See Appendix B for program listing.) Results are shown in panel 3 of Table 3. For the most part the results are quite similar to those in panels 1 and 2. The big difference is in the effect of employment status, which is now clearly the most important variable in the model. Exponentiating the coefficient of −1.397 yields .25, which says that the hazard of arrest for those who were working was only one fourth the hazard of those who were not working.

**Problems with Time-Varying
Explanatory Variables**

A word of warning is in order here. Regardless of the computer program, estimation of proportional hazards models with time-varying explanatory variables can enormously increase computational costs. In this example, for instance, the CPU time increased by a factor of 10 with the inclusion of just one time-varying explanatory variable. Moreover, setting up the model may not be straightforward. With the exception of variables that are very simple functions of time itself, BMDP2L requires the inclusion of a FORTRAN subroutine to define the time-varying variables. Procedures for doing this are not well documented.

Another possible complication in the estimation of models with time-varying explanatory variables involves the frequency with which those variables are measured. Strictly speaking, estimation of such models requires that for each time that an event occurs, values of the explanatory variables must be known for all individuals at risk at that time. Thus, if an event occurred at time 10, and 15 individuals were at risk at that time, the values of the explanatory variables at time 10 must be known for all 15 individuals. Typically, that would require that the explanatory variables be measured continuously over time.

In practice, however, time-varying explanatory variables are usually measured at regular intervals. In the example just considered, employment status was known for each week of observation. That created no problem because the time of arrest was measured in weeks. Difficulties arise when time of event occurrence is measured more precisely than the interval at which the explanatory variables are measured. For example, event times may be measured in days but the values of the explanatory variables may be known only at the beginning of each month.

In such cases, some ad hoc procedure will be necessary to estimate the values of the explanatory variables at the times of events. The simplest approach is to use the value closest in time to the event time as the estimated value. A better method is to use linear interpolation, which is equivalent to weighted averaging. Suppose, for example, that the values of an explanatory variable x are known at time 10 and time 20 but an event occurs at time 13. An estimate of x(13) is given by x(10)(.7) + x(20)(.3). For a discussion of these and other methods, see Tuma (1982).

Adequacy of the Proportional Hazards Model

Many researchers worry about whether their data satisfy the proportional hazards assumption. For those with such concerns, there are ways of both assessing the validity of this assumption and altering the model to correct for violations. Before discussing these methods, however, let us consider the possibility that these worries may be exaggerated. As models go, the proportional hazards model is extraordinarily general and nonrestrictive—the main reason for its great popularity. Even when the proportional hazards assumption is violated, it is often a satisfactory approximation. Those who are concerned about misspecification would usually do better to focus on the possibilities of omitted explanatory variables, measurement error in the explanatory variables, and nonindependence of censoring and the occurence of events.

With that in mind, let us proceed to talk about nonproportional hazards. What does it mean to say that hazards are not proportional? As noted earlier, models with time-varying explanatory variables do not have proportional hazards, but there are other ways in which this can occur. When the dependent variable is the logarithm of the hazard, the hazards are not proportional if there is an *interaction* between time and one or more explanatory variables, e.g.,

$$\log h(t) = a(t) + bx + cxt \qquad [13]$$

This model differs from the usual model by including the product of x and t as one of the explanatory variables. If c is positive, we can say that the effect of time on the hazard increases linearly as x increases. Alternatively, we can say that the effect of x on the hazard goes up linearly with time. Hence, the hazards are not proportional if the effect of some explanatory variable on the hazard is different at different points in time.

There are other ways of expressing interaction, of course, but the partial likelihood method can estimate a broad class of these by including additional variables in the model. Specifically, it can estimate models of the form

$$\log h(t) = a(t) + bx + c\, g(x,t) \qquad [14]$$

where g(x,t) is some nonlinear function of x and t with known parameters. One simply computes g(x,t) for each event time t and includes this in the model as a time-varying explanatory variable. Thus, one very good way of testing for nonproportionality is to estimate models of this form, and then test whether the coefficient c differs significantly from zero. If it does, then one has already solved the problem by estimating the extended model.

A limitation of this approach is that not all partial likelihood programs allow time-dependent explanatory variables. Moreover, estimation of such models tends to be expensive. There is a much cheaper graphical method that works well when time interacts with a categorical (nominal) variable, or one that can be treated as categorical. In this method, a certain function of time (the log-log survival function) is plotted for subsamples corresponding to the different levels of the categorical variable. If the categorical variable is sex, for example, one plot is produced for males and another plot is produced for females. These plots should be roughly parallel if the proportional hazards assumption is satisfied. (For further information see Lawless, 1982, and the BMDP2L manual.)

If this graphical test provides evidence against the proportional hazards assumption, there is a method called "stratification" that allows for nonproportionality. It is much cheaper than using time-varying explanatory variables. The basic idea is to divide the sample into strata according to the values of the categorical variable that interacts with time. A separate model is then postulated for each stratum.

Suppose, for example, that males and females are thought to have nonproportional hazards. We then specify two models:

$$\text{males: } \log h(t) = a_1(t) + b_1 x_1 + b_2 x_2 + \ldots$$

$$\text{females: } \log h(t) = a_2(t) + b_1 x_1 + b_2 x_2 + \ldots \qquad [15]$$

These models share the same set of b coefficients but each has a different (but unspecified) function of time. Both models can be estimated simultaneously using the partial likelihood method. Stratification is available in the BMDP2L program, the 1983 version of the SAS PHGLM procedure, and in the SURVREG program (Preston and Clarkson, 1983).

Another approach to checking the adequacy of the model is the examination of residuals. Methods for calculating residuals from the proportional hazards model have been proposed by Kay (1977) and Schoenfeld (1982). Kay's formula has been incorporated into the BMDP2L program, which also plots those residuals in such a way that deviations from a straight line represent a failure of the model. Unfortunately, a recent investigation (Crowley and Storer, 1983) raises questions about the diagnostic value of such plots.

Those accustomed to multiple regression will undoubtedly wish that there were something like R^2 for proportional hazards models. Harrel (1980) has developed an R^2 analog for these models, and has incorporated it into the SAS supplementary procedure PHGLM. From his description, however, it is not clear that this is the most appropriate analog, and others may yet be developed. In any case, it must be emphasized that such a statistic does *not* measure how well the assumptions of the model are satisfied by the data. As in ordinary multiple regression, a low R^2 is quite compatible with a model that is perfectly specified, and a high R^2 can be found for models that are grossly misspecified. Such statistics only tell one how much variation in the dependent variable is attributable to variations in the explanatory variables.

Choice of Origin of the Time Scale

One aspect of model choice that has been implicit to this point is the question of when time begins. While this question is relevant to both parametric and semiparametric models, a discussion has been postponed until now because the proportional hazards model offers a wider range of possibilities. In the recidivism example, the origin of the time scale was relatively unambiguous. The date of release is a natural starting point for calculating time of first arrest after release. Similarly, if one is estimating models for the hazard of divorce, the date of marriage is a natural starting point for calculating time of divorce.

There are many cases, however, in which the origin of the time scale will not be so clear. Even in seemingly straightforward examples, moreover, there is room for disagreement. In formulating a proportional hazards model for recidivism, for instance, one could let the hazard be a function of the person's age or calendar time rather than time since release. Age and calendar time are also possible time scales for the hazard for divorce.

There would be no difficulty in estimating such models by partial likelihood, but would it be reasonable to do so? That depends on substantive considerations. If the hazard is known to depend strongly on age but only weakly on time since some other starting point, then age would probably be the most appropriate way to define the time scale. Or if the hazard is thought to vary greatly with historical conditions that affect all sample members in the same way, then calendar time might be the best time scale.

In theory, one could formulate and estimate proportional hazards models in which the hazard depended arbitrarily on two or more time scales. In practice, this requires very large samples or special conditions described by Tuma (1982). Even when this approach is not possible, however, one can always explicitly introduce different time scales as explanatory variables. For example, in estimating a proportional hazards model for divorce in which the hazard varies arbitrarily with duration of marriage, one could also include calendar year, age of husband, and age of wife as explanatory variables. If any of these variables has a nonlinear effect (on the log of the hazard), it is necessary to specify the variable as a time-varying explanatory variable. When the effect is linear (on the log of the hazard), however, it is sufficient to measure the variable at the beginning of the principal time scale, in this case the beginning of the marriage.[6] Another example is provided by Table 3 where age at release is included as an explanatory variable.

Partial Likelihood for Discrete-Time Data

The discussion of the partial likelihood method has assumed that time is measured on a continuous scale and that, as a consequence, two events cannot occur at exactly the same time. In practice, time is always measured in discrete units, however small, and many data sets will contain "ties"—two or more individuals experiencing events at apparently the same time. Thus, in the recidivism example where time was measured in weeks, there were several weeks in which two or more persons were arrested.

To handle such data, both the model and the partial likelihood method must be modified to some degree. The model proposed by Cox (1972) for data with ties is just the logit-linear model of equation 3 in Chapter 1. This model is attractive because, as the discrete-time units get smaller and smaller, it converges to the proportional hazards model (Thompson, 1977).

The method of partial likelihood may be used to estimate this model but, if the number of ties is at all large, the computational requirements are gargantuan. To avoid this, a number of approximations have been proposed, the most widely accepted of which is Breslow's (1974). This formula has been incorporated into most programs for partial likelihood estimation including all those mentioned here. When there are no tied data, Breslow's formula reduces to the usual partial likelihood for continuous-time data. Thus, such programs can be used for either continuous- or discrete-time data, and there is usually no need for the researcher to be concerned about the occurrence of ties.

42

This approach is not fool-proof, however. If the number of events occurring at most time points is large relative to the number at risk (say, 50 percent or more), the Breslow approximation will be poor (Farewell and Prentice, 1980). In such situations, it would be better to use the discrete-time estimation method described in Chapter 1.

5. MULTIPLE KINDS OF EVENTS

In the previous chapters all the events under study were treated as though they were exactly alike. Thus, in Chapter 2 we did not distinguish among different kinds of job changes, and in Chapter 3 all arrests were treated the same. Often this will not do. In some cases, lumping together different kinds of events may be completely inappropriate. Even when it is appropriate, however, a more refined analysis in which different kinds of events are examined separately is often desirable.

Fortunately, no new methodology is required. The methods already discussed for single kinds of events can also be used with multiple kinds of events; they just have to be applied in more complicated ways. Unfortunately, there is still much confusion surrounding this topic, and I believe that it is largely due to the fact that there are multiple kinds of "multiple kinds of events." This phrase really describes several quite different situations, each requiring a different approach to analysis.

A Classification of Multiple Kinds of Events

The first contribution of this chapter will be a classification of these different situations. For simplicity let us assume that there are only two kinds of events. Generalizations to more than two kinds of events should be apparent. (Usually, the number of different kinds of events will be a somewhat arbitrary choice of the analyst.) Also, we shall continue to assume that events are not repeated, leaving that complication for the next chapter.

The first major class may be described as follows:

I. The occurrence or nonoccurrence of an event is determined by one causal process; given that an event occurs, a second causal process determines which type occurs.

It is easy to think of examples that fall in this class. Consider the event of buying a car, and suppose we distinguish buying an American car from buying a foreign car. It is implausible that distinct causal processes lead to each of these two types of events. Rather, one first decides to buy a car; then, independent of that decision, one decides whether that car is to be an American or foreign car. It is likely that rather different explanatory variables affect each of these decisions. Another example is provided by the event of a visit to a physician, where we distinguish visits to osteopaths from visits to M.D.s. Again it is most plausible that the decision to visit some kind of physician is distinct from the decision of what kind to visit. It doesn't matter which precedes the other; the important ingredient here is that one decision is distinct from the other.

For this class of "multiple kinds of events," the appropriate strategy for analysis is one that is isomorphic to the structure of the decision-making process. One first uses the event history methods described in the previous chapters to model the occurrence of the event, making no distinction between event types. Then, looking only at those individuals for whom events occurred, one uses an appropriate technique for modelling the causal process which determined the type of event. An obvious choice would be binomial logit analysis (or multinomial logit analysis if there are more than two types).

The second broad class of "multiple kinds of events" consists of those situations in which the following is true:

II. The occurrence of each event type has a different causal structure.

A different causal structure means either that different explanatory variables affect the occurrence of each event type, or that the same explanatory variables have different coefficients or different functional forms. Rather than providing examples of this general class, let us proceed immediately to the four subclasses. We shall also postpone discussing the method of analysis until all four subclasses have been described.

IIa. The occurrence of one event type removes the individual from risk of the other event type.

Often described as "competing risks," this class has received much attention from biostatisticians and demographers. The classic example is death from competing causes. Clearly there are different causal processes leading to death from heart disease and death from cancer. Yet a person who dies of heart disease is no longer at risk of dying of cancer, and vice versa. There are also many examples in the social sciences. It is very likely, for instance, that voluntary job terminations occur as a result of different causal processes than involuntary job terminations, if only because different decision makers are involved in the two types of termination. Yet once a person quits a job, he or she is no longer at risk of being fired. And once fired, a person no longer has the option of quitting. A similar example is marital dissolution, where divorce is distinguished from death of a spouse.

IIb. The occurrence of one type of event removes the individual from observation of other event types.

In studies of human migration, one might distinguish moves within a country from moves between countries. It would not be uncommon for individuals to be lost to further study if they moved out of a country. Even though such an individual is no longer observed, he or she would still be at risk of a within-country move.

This example is a asymmetric in that individuals who move within a country are still at risk of a between-country move and may continue to be observed. It is easy to imagine symmetric cases, however. For example, a study of criminal recidivism may distinguish arrests for violent and nonviolent crimes. If the follow-up does not continue past the first arrest, then the study would fall into class IIb.

IIc. The occurrence on one kind of event affects neither the risk of occurrence nor the observation of other kinds of events.

While there are probably no two kinds of events that are absolutely unrelated, there are many cases that for all practical purposes, can be treated as if there were no relationship. Suppose, for example, that one event is voting in an election and the other is a divorce. Or perhaps one kind of event is getting a raise and the other kind is having a car accident.

IId. The occurrence of one kind of event raises or lowers (but not to zero) the hazard of the other kind of event.

It is easy to think of examples in this class. For unmarried women, getting pregnant increases the hazard of marriage. Marriage, in turn, increases the hazard of giving birth. Getting promoted reduces the hazard of quitting a job. Becoming employed reduces the hazard of being arrested.

Estimation for Multiple Kinds of Events

We now consider how to deal with these four subclasses. Class IIc is easy. If the occurrence of an event has no effect either on the observation or risk of occurrence of another event, then the first event can be completely ignored in studying the second event. Thus, this class is effectively the same as that discussed in the previous chapters.

On the other hand, if the occurrence of one event raises or lowers the hazard of the occurrence of the other event (class IId), then surely the first event must be taken into account in studying the second event. Again, however, we already have a method for doing this. The trick is to use the occurrence of the first kind of event to define a time-varying explanatory variable in the analysis of the second kind of event. Thus, in the biochemistry example, a time-varying dummy variable indicating a change in rank was used to predict the occurrence of an employer change. Similarly, in the analysis of arrests, a dummy variable was included to indicate whether or not the person was employed in each week. Alternatively, one could create a variable measuring the length of time since employment began. In fact, there is no reason why both variables could not be included as explanatory variables.

Class IIb is quite similar to what has already been described as censoring: An individual is removed from observation at some point prior to the occurrence of the event of interest. The difference here is that censoring is now an event in its own right. Despite this difference, the best available analytic strategy remains the same. Each event type is analyzed separately using the models and methods of the previous chapter. Events that remove the individual from observation are treated just as if the individual were censored at that point in time. For example, in analyzing the causes of within-country migration, individuals who made between-country moves (and hence could not be followed up) would be considered censored at the time of the between-country move.

Although I know of no better way to handle this situation, it is not entirely unproblematic. Recall that all the event history methods described so far require that censoring times be independent of event times. That requirement still stands even though censoring is now a distinct type of event. Thus, in the migration analysis just proposed, it must be assumed that times of between-country moves are independent of times of within-country moves, an assumption that may not be plausible. While it is possible to formulate and estimate models that build in some dependence, it is impossible to distinguish them empirically from models that specify independence.

Class IIa (competing risks), in which the occurrence of an event removes the individual from risk of other events, is the one most commonly discussed in the event history literature. Accordingly, it is the one to which we shall devote the most attention. It is superficially similar to class IIb, just considered, and indeed the basic message is the same. Methods for single kinds of events may be applied separately to each kind of event. In analyzing each event, the individual is treated as censored at the occurrence of any other kind of event. Because of the importance of this result, let us spend a little time on the background and the argument. Then we can proceed to an example.

Models for Competing Risks

There are several ways to approach the problem of competing risks, but the most common is to begin by defining what are known as "type-specific" (or "cause-specific") hazard functions. Suppose there are m different kinds of events and let $j = 1, \ldots, m$ be the running index distinguishing the different kinds of event. Let $P_j(t, t + s)$ be the probability that event type j occurs in the interval between t and t + s, given that the individual is at risk at time t. Note that the individual is *not* at risk at time t if any of the m events have occurred prior to t.

The type-specific hazard rate is then defined as

$$h_j(t) = \lim_{s \to 0} P_j(t, t + s)/s \qquad [16]$$

Thus, each event type has its own hazard function. It can be shown that the overall hazard function h(t), which is the hazard for the occurrence of any of the m events, is just the sum of all the type-specific hazard functions.

For each of these type-specific hazard functions, one can develop a model for dependence on time and on the explanatory variables. Any of the models already discussed would be reasonable candidates. These models may be very much alike, or they can be completely different for each kind of event. In any case, it can be shown that the likelihood function (which is maximized in maximum likelihood estimation) for the data can be factored into a separate likelihood function for each kind of event. Moreover, those factors look exactly like likelihood functions for single kinds of events with all other events treated as censored. Thus maximum likelihood or partial likelihood estimation can be done separately for each event type, using the methods described in the previous chapters. That does not mean that estimating separate models for each type of event is the only way to proceed. In fact the RATE program does simultaneous estimation for multiple kinds of events. The importance of this result is that, at a theoretical level, there is nothing really new about models for competing risks. And at a practical level, estimating models separately for each kind of event gives one much greater flexibility and control over the kinds of models estimated. For example, one could specify a Weibull regression model for one kind of event and a Gompertz regression model for another kind of event. Or more likely, the models for different kinds of events might have different explanatory variables or the same explanatory variables transformed in different ways. Most importantly, one can ignore event types that are of little or no interest. In a study of marital dissolution, for example, if one is only interested in the causes of divorce, it is not necessary to estimate models for both divorce and death of a spouse.

An Empirical Example of Competing Risks

For an example of a competing risks analysis, we again consider data from a study of criminal recidivism. Known as TARP (Rossi et al., 1980), the study was a large-scale replication of the experiment described and analyzed in Chapter 3. Approximately 4000 inmates released from prisons in Texas and Georgia were randomly assigned to experimental treatments involving various levels of financial aid and job search assistance. They were followed for one year after release, when a search was made of public records for any arrests which occurred during the follow-up year. For this example, the analysis is restricted to 955 Georgia convicts interviewed during the follow-up year. The event of interest is the first arrest to occur after release, so that those with no arrests during the one-year period are treated as censored.

Various types of arrests will be distinguished, depending on the type of crime allegedly committed. In one phase of the analysis, we shall distinguish crimes against property (robbery, burglary, larceny, and so on) from all others. In a later phase, we shall further subdivide nonproperty crimes into violent and nonviolent crimes.

Continuous-time methods are most appropriate since the exact day of each arrest is known. Using the SAS PHGLM procedure, we shall estimate proportional hazard models of the form

$$\log h_j(t) = a_j(t) + b_{j1}x_1 + b_{j2}x_2 + \ldots \qquad [17]$$

where the j subscripts indicate that there is a different set of coefficients and a different arbitrary function of time for each arrest type. Explanatory variables include education, marital status at time of release, age at release, age at earliest known arrest, sex, number of previous convictions for crimes against persons, number of previous convictions for crimes against property, a dummy variable indicating whether the incarceration was for a crime against persons, a dummy variable indicating whether the incarceration was for a property crime, and a dummy variable indicating whether or not the person was released on parole. Tha analysis is simplified by the fact that none of these is a time-varying explanatory variable.

We begin by estimating a model which does not distinguish different kinds of arrests. There were 340 persons with at least one arrest, so the remaining 615 persons with no arrests were censored at 365 days. The estimated coefficients are given in Table 4, column 1. Only four of the 11 explanatory variables are significant at the .05 level or beyond: age at initial arrest, number of previous property convictions, incarceration for a property offense, and release on parole. Note that the dummy variable for financial aid does not have a significant effect, and even has a sign opposite that which was expected. Thus it appears that financial aid is not effective in reducing recidivism.

This initial model is unsatisfactory, however, because theory suggests that financial aid should reduce property offenses but not other offenses. It is also possible that other variables may have different effects on different kinds of arrests. To examine this possibility, we subdivide arrests into 192 property arrests and 148 nonproperty arrests, and then estimate a separate proportional hazards model for each type of arrest. When estimating the model for property arrests, persons whose first arrest was for a nonproperty arrest are treated as censored at the time of that arrest. Similarly, in the model for nonproperty arrests, property arrests are equivalent to censoring.

This may seem like an artificial example of competing risks since, after the first arrest, the subjects continued to be observed and at risk of both kinds of events. It could, in fact, be reasonably argued that the example most appropriately falls into class IId rather than class IIa. Nevertheless, if one believes that the first arrest after release represents the crucial step in return to a criminal career, it is reasonable to focus only on that arrest. If the first arrest is for a property arrest, then the individual is no longer at risk of a first arrest for a nonproperty arrest, and vice versa. In the next chapter we shall see evidence that later arrests *are* different from first arrests.

TABLE 4
Estimates of Proportional Hazards Models for Different Arrest Types

Explanatory Variables	1 All Arrests	2 Property	3 Nonproperty	4 Violent	5 Other
Education	−.022	−.006	−.033	−.086	.015
Financial aid (D)[a]	.108	.215	−.050	−.254	.140
Imprisoned for crime against person (D)	.080	.062	.087	.280	−−.037
Imprisoned for crime against property (D)	.449**	.889**	−.005	.300	−.221
Number of convictions for crimes against persons	−.124	−.089	−.145	.320	−1.29
Number of convictions for crimes against property	.232**	.242**	.226*	.361*	.092
Paroled (D)	.273*	.167	.414*	.173	.620*
Male (D)	.271	.203	.322	.214	.427
Age at earliest arrest	−.043**	−.051**	−.035*	−.023	−.045
Married (D)	.053	−.036	.167	.124	.187
Age at release	−.009	−.010	−.007	−.015	.000
N of arrests	340	192	148	69	78
N	955	955	955	955	955

a. (D) indicates dummy variable.
*Significant at .05 level.
**Significant at .01 level.

Results from estimating models for the two kinds of arrests are shown in columns 2 and 3 of Table 4. The effects of age at initial arrest and number of previous property convictions are approximately the same for each type of arrest. On the other hand, release on parole has a significant effect on nonproperty arrests but no effect on property arrests. Moreover, previous incarceration for a property crime substantially increases the risk of being arrested for a property crime but not for a nonproperty crime. Financial aid has no significant effect on either type of arrest.

Although we could stop the analysis at this point, further insight is obtained by subdividing the nonproperty arrests into two categories: violent crimes against persons and all other offenses. (This residual category consists, for the most part, of such relatively minor offenses as possession of marijuana, carrying a concealed weapon, and "neglect of family.") A separate model is then estimated for each type of arrest, with results shown in columns 4 and 5 of Table 4. Note that only one variable has a significant effect for each arrest type. This is a consequence of the fact that overall significance levels will go down as the number of events becomes a smaller proportion of the total sample size. What is important here is that the effect of release on parole is large and significant for the "other" category but small and nonsignificant for violent crimes against persons. Similarly, while the number of previous property convictions has a significant effect on the hazard for violent offenses, it has no effect on other types of nonproperty offenses.

We see, then, that distinguishing different kinds of events can lead to different conclusions about the effects of explanatory variables. Similarly, the failure to distinguish among event types may produce misleading results. For example, in the model for all kinds of arrests, we found that those released on parole had a higher hazard for being arrested. Nevertheless, when we focused on specific types of events, the effect of parole status was significant only for relatively minor offenses.

Dependence Among Different Kinds of Events

The approach we have just described and applied for class IIa, competing risks, has one very important property. The type-specific hazard functions are defined in such a way that it is unnecessary to make any assumptions about dependence or independence among different kinds of events. To understand what this means, consider again the example of job terminations where we distinguish voluntary terminations from involuntary terminations. The two types would be dependent if, for example, persons who knew they were likely to be fired were more likely to quit, possibly to avoid the stigma of being fired. Or it could work the other way. Persons who wanted to quit might arrange to be fired in order to collect unemployment insurance. Neither case poses any problems for the kind of model which we have just considered.

While this is an attractive feature, it can be argued that the model solves the problem of dependence versus independence by simply defining it away. In fact, there are other approaches to competing risks in which the problem of dependence is crucial and, in some respects, insoluble. It can be shown, for example, that it is impossible to distinguish empirically models in which different kinds of events are dependent from a model in which they are independent (Tsiatis, 1975). While the mathematics of these different approaches is thoroughly developed, the interpretation and implications for empirical research are still controversial. (For a detailed discussion, see Kalbfleisch and Prentice, 1980: Ch. 7.)

6. REPEATED EVENTS

Most events studied by social scientists are repeatable, and most event history data contain repeated events for each individual. Examples include job changes, births, marriages, divorces, arrests, convictions, and visits to a physician. Unfortunately, the enormous literature on event history methods that has come out of biostatistics contains only a handful of articles on the analysis of repeated events (e.g., Gail, Santner, and Brown, 1980; Prentice, Williams, and Peterson, 1981). As already noted, this is a consequence of the fact that the events of greatest interest in biomedical research are deaths. While sociologists (Tuma, Hannan, and Groeneveld, 1979) and economists (Flinn and Heckman, 1982a, 1982b) have made some progress in this area, there is still much to be done in the way of developing methods that are suitable for repeated events.

One approach that is sometimes appropriate is to conduct a separate analysis for each successive event using any of the methods already discussed. In a study of marital fertility, for example, one could estimate a model for the interval between marriage and first birth, a second model for the interval between first and second birth, and so on. This approach requires no special assumptions, and is especially useful if one expects the model to differ from one event to another. On the other hand, if the process is essentially the same across successive events, doing a separate analysis for each event is both tedious and statistically inefficient.

A Simple Approach

In this chapter we shall focus on a second approach that avoids these difficulties by treating each interval between events for each individual as a separate observation. These intervals (sometimes referred to as spells) are then pooled over all individuals. At this point any of the methods described in the previous chapters can be applied. Although this approach is not entirely satisfactory from the viewpoint of statistical theory, we shall postpone a discussion of those problems until later in this chapter. There are also a number of possible complications not discussed in earlier chapters.

To simplify the discussion, let us assume that the repeated events are of a single kind. (In the next chapter we shall consider models that incorporate both multiple kinds of events and repeated events.) We begin by extending the empirical example discussed in Chapter 5. Recall

TABLE 5
Frequency Distribution for Arrests

Number of Arrests	Number of Persons
0	622
1	213
2	85
3	25
4	9
5	5
6	2

that the sample consisted of approximately 1000 inmates released from Georgia state prisons who were observed for one year after their release. In the previous analysis, the event of interest was the first arrest that occurred after release. As Table 5 shows, however, many of the subjects were arrested more than once during the one-year follow-up period, and to ignore the later arrests seems wasteful of information. It also raises the question of whether the causal process differed for earlier and later arrests.

To incorporate these additional arrests into an event history analysis, let us divide each individual's one-year follow-up period into intervals, using the observed arrests as the dividing points. Consider, for example, a person with two arrests that occurred at times marked by Xs on the line below:

|————————X————————————————X————|
0   1 year

With two arrests there are three intervals, the last of which is censored by the end of the observation period. Similarly, a person with four arrests would have five intervals, the last of which is censored. Thus, every individual has exactly one censored interval, and may also have one or more uncensored intervals. For this sample, the 961 persons had a total of 1492 intervals, and, of course, 961 of those were censored.

Treating each of those intervals as a separate observation and pooling all intervals, we now reestimate the proportional hazards model corresponding to column 1 of Table 4. Results are shown in Table 6, column 1. Notice that the effective number of observations is increased by about 50 percent, and the number of observed arrests is increased by over 60

TABLE 6
Estimates of Proportional Hazards Models for Repeated Arrests

Explanatory Variables	All Arrests 1 b	t	2 b	t	Second or Later Arrests 3 b	t
Education	−.008	−.35	−.010	.45	.020	.52
Financial aid (D)[a]	.150	1.69	.136	1.54	.142	.95
Imprisoned for crime against person (D)	.173	1.25	.153	1.11	.207	.92
Imprisoned for crime against property (D)	.367	3.17**	.336	2.88**	.090	.45
Number of convictions for crimes against persons	.051	.10	−.002	.00	.162	.75
Number of convictions for crimes against property	.183	3.27**	.155	2.73**	.061	.66
Paroled (D)	.341	3.65**	.312	3.31**	.297	1.75
Male (D)	.054	.26	.076	.37	−.134	.45
Age at earliest arrest	−.043	4.20**	−.038	3.73**	−.022	1.27
Married (D)	.160	1.50	.151	1.42	.293	1.71
Age at release	−.008	1.17	−.008	1.14	−.003	.30
Number of prior intervals	–	–	.197	2.59**	.087	.96
Time since release	–	–	.017	2.05*	−.001	1.01
N or arrests	549		549		203	
N	1492		1492		531	

a. (D) indicates dummy variable.
*Significant at .05 level.
**Significant at .01 level.

percent. It is reasonable to expect, then, that the new estimates should have smaller standard errors and, hence, larger t-statistics. Indeed, although the basic pattern of results is the same, we do find somewhat larger t-statistics when all the arrests are included. In fact, the positive effect of financial aid is now marginally significant by a one-tailed test.

Problems with Repeated Events

While the method just described is straightforward and intuitively appealing, it requires that one make a number of assumptions that may well be problematic. First, one must assume that the dependence of the hazard on time since last event has the same form for each successive event. Recall that in a proportional hazards model,

$$\log h(t) = a(t) + b_1 x_1 + b_2 x_2 + \ldots \qquad [18]$$

where t is the length of time since the last event and a(t) is an unspecified function of time. Even though it is unspecified, a(t) must be the same function for the first arrest, the second arrest, and so on. Or if one assumes that intervals have a Weibull distribution, that distribution must have the same shape parameter for each successive interval. If there is reason to be suspicious of this assumption, the proportional hazards model can be modified to make it unnecessary. The basic idea is to let the function a(t) be different for each successive interval, while forcing the b coefficients to be the same. Such a model can be readily estimated using the method of stratification discussed in Chapter 4.

A second assumption implicit in this method is that, for each individual, the multiple intervals must be statistically independent. In general, we would expect that people who are frequently arrested (i.e., have short intervals) will continue to be frequently arrested. This does not violate the assumption of independence, so long as that dependence is fully accounted for by the explanatory variables included in the model.

In most cases, however, there will be good reason to think that the independence assumption is false, at least to some degree. The consequences of violating this assumption have not been studied, but analogies with linear regression suggest that (a) the coefficient estimates will still be asymptotically unbiased and (b) standard error estimates will be biased downward. Work is now being done on ways to relax the independence assumption by introducing a random disturbance term that is correlated across intervals (Flinn and Heckman, 1982a, 1982b). This approach has not progressed to the point where the new methods can be generally recommended, however.

In the meantime, there are some things that can be done to minimize the consequences of violating the independence assumption. The basic idea is to include in the model additional explanatory variables that tap characteristics of the individual's prior event history. The simplest such variables are the number of events prior to the interval in question, and the length of the previous interval, set to zero when no previous interval is observed.

Another approach to the problem of dependence is to modify the estimated standard errors so that they reflect the number of individuals rather than the number of intervals. Let n and N be the number of individuals and the number of intervals, respectively. The standard errors may be adjusted upward by multiplying each one by the square root of N/n. Similarly, the t-statistics may be adjusted downward by multiplying each one by the square root of n/N. The rationale for this adjustment is that, if intervals are highly dependent, the multiple intervals for a single individual are redundant—an individual with many intervals is not contributing much more information than an individual with just one interval. The approach is highly conservative, however, and probably results in overestimates of the true standard errors.

A third limitation of models for repeated events considered thus far is that the hazard rate is expressed as a function of the time since the last event. While this is by far the most common specification, there are often situations in which it is more plausible to let the hazard vary as a function of age or time since some common starting point. In studies of fertility, for example, age may have stronger effects on the hazard for a birth than length of time since the previous birth. We have discussed the problem of starting points in Chapter 4, but some additional remarks are in order here. First, the question of origin of the time scale is *always* ambiguous in the case of repeated events and should always be given careful consideration. Second, models for repeated events in which the hazard depends on time since some fixed starting point may be inconvenient to estimate. Consider, for example, the proportional hazards model in equation 18 where we now consider t to be time since release from prison rather than time since the last event. Such a model can, in principle, be estimated by the partial likelihood method, but the commonly available partial likelihood programs do not have that capability.[7] See Prentice, Williams, and Peterson (1981) for further details. Perhaps the best approach, at present, is to include age or time since some other point as an explanatory variable in models that allow the hazard to vary with time since the last event.

Extending the Recidivism Example

Let us now return to the recidivism example to incorporate some of the new possibilities just discussed. In panel 2 of Table 6, estimates are given for a model that includes number of prior arrests and length of time from release to the beginning of each interval. Both of these new variables are statistically significant. The positive effect of number of prior arrests indicates, as expected, that those with many arrests have a higher hazard for arrest at subsequent points in time. The positive effect of time since release indicates a tendency for the hazard to increase over the one-year observation period. The inclusion of these variables somewhat attenuates the coefficients and t-statistics for the other variables in the model. In fact, the t-statistics are about the same as those for the model which only examined the first arrest. Some attenuation is to be expected since the violation of the independence assumption is likely to lead to inflated t-statistics.

When corrections are introduced for possible violations of assumptions, it appears that not much has been gained by analyzing all arrests rather than just the first arrest. This is surprising since the inclusion of the additional arrests ought to have yielded diminished standard errors and, hence, increased t-statistics. One possible explanation is that the causal process may be somewhat different for arrests after the first. To examine this possibility, the second model was reestimated after excluding all the intervals from release to first arrest. This left 531 intervals of which 231 ended in arrest. Results are shown in panel 3 of Table 6. With the exception of parole status, none of the explanatory variables even approaches statistical significance. It is reasonable to expect *some* decline in significance level since the effective sample size has been reduced greatly. Nevertheless, the coefficients of the formerly significant variables are also greatly attenuated, suggesting that there has been a real decline in the effects of these variables for later arrests. We shall not speculate on the reasons for this decline.

Left Censoring

Before leaving the topic of repeated events, let us consider one further problem that is quite common but did not occur in this particular example. The problem is often referred to as "left censoring," but it is worth noting that biostatisticians mean something quite different when they use this term.[8]

Suppose that a sample of people is observed over a five-year period, and the event of interest is a job change. During that five-year period, the pattern for a particular individual with three job changes might look like this:

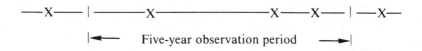

where X denotes the occurrence of a job change and the two extreme Xs (to the right and left of the vertical lines) refer to events that are not observed. The three observed events divide the five-year period into four intervals. The last interval is clearly censored and the middle two intervals are clearly uncensored. The first interval is problematic, however. Although it ends with an event, the interval is still censored because the time of the preceding event is unknown.

The consequences of left censoring depend on the model being estimated. If the model specifies a hazard rate that does not depend on time (an exponential model in the continuous case), there is no problem whatever. One simply treats the initial censored interval as if it began at the beginning of the observation period. Similarly, there is no inherent difficulty if the hazard rate depends on age, except for the computational problem noted above.

Dependence on the time since the last event poses serious problems, however, because the time since the last event is not known. Treating the interval as if it began at the beginning of the observation period will undoubtedly introduce some bias. Flinn and Heckman (1982a, 1982b) discuss several possible solutions to this problem, but all are computationally cumbersome and depend on somewhat arbitrary assumptions. The safest approach is simply to discard the initially censored intervals. While this represents a loss of information, it should not lead to any biases.

7. CHANGE OF STATES

In this chapter we shall consider a class of models that allows for both multiple kinds of events and repeated events. This class includes all the previously discussed continuous-time models as special cases. Known as Markov renewal or semi-Markov models, these models have been previously described in the social science literature by Coleman (1981), Tuma, Hannan, and Groeneveld (1979), and others.

Markov models describe processes in which individuals are in one of a set of mutually exclusive and exhaustive states at any point in time. For example, in applying their model to the study of marital status, Tuma et al. (1979) distinguished three states: married, unmarried, and attrited. Knoke (1982) used a version of the model to study forms of city government: commission, council-manager, mayor-council. Diprete (1981) studied employment versus unemployment. The set of possible states is often called the state space. For the model to be of any interest, it must be possible to make transitions between at least some of the states, and it is assumed that those transitions can occur at any point in time.

These state transitions are equivalent to the "events" discussed in the preceding chapters. In fact, any kind of event considered thus far can be thought of as a transition between states, although this may sometimes be a bit artificial. For example, an arrest can be thought of as a transition from having had, say, four arrests to having had five arrests. Similarly, the birth of a child is a move from n children to n + 1 children.

Transition Rates

Transitions among these states are controlled by a set of unobserved *transition rates*, which are defined as follows. Let $P_{ij}(t, t + s)$ be the probability that an individual who is in state i at time t will be in state j at time t + s. Then the transition rates, denoted by $r_{ij}(t)$, are given by

$$r_{ij}(t) = \lim_{s \to 0} P_{ij}(t, t + s)/s \qquad [19]$$

Notice the similarity between equation 19 and the definition of the type-specific hazard functions in equation 16. In fact, the type-specific hazard functions are just transition rates for the special case in which all individuals begin in the same origin state. To put it another way, transition rates can be regarded as type-specific hazard functions in which events are distinguished both by origin and destination states.

The transition rates, in turn, are allowed to depend on time and the explanatory variables, with the most common functional form being

$$\log r_{ij}(t) = a_{ij}(t - t') + b_{ij} \, x \qquad [20]$$

where x represents a set (vector) of explanatory variables, b_{ij} represents a set (vector) of coefficients, t' is the time of the last transition, and $a_{ij}(t - t')$ is some function (as yet unspecified) of the time since the last transition. The function $a_{ij}(t - t')$ is often constrained to be a constant a_{ij}, which implies that the time between transitions is exponentially distributed. Implicit in the model are the assumptions that time intervals between events are independent and, for each ij combination, identically distributed.

This model, or variations thereof, can be estimated with a variety of forms of data (Coleman, 1981). Nevertheless, the best form of data is clearly an event history in which both the timing and the type of all transitions are recorded. Tuma's RATE program is designed to estimate this model directly using event history data. In fact, however, virtually any computer program for doing event history analysis can estimate at least some version of this model. This chapter will show how to estimate equation 20 using a standard program for estimating proportional hazards models.

Analysis may be accomplished through the following steps:

(1) Break each individual's event history into a set of intervals between events.

(2) Separate these intervals into groups according to origin state.

(3) For each origin state, estimate models for multiple kinds of events, specifically for class IIa (competing risks). Each destination state corresponds to a different event type. As in Chapter 5, a separate model may be estimated for each destination state, treating all other destinations as censored at the end of the interval.

An Analysis of Job Changes

To illustrate this procedure, we shall analyze data on job changes of 477 physicists surveyed in 1966. (For a detailed description of the data see Hagstrom, 1974.) Information on job histories of these physicists was obtained from *American Men and Women of Science* (Cattel Press, 1966). Data were available on each job held by each physicist from the receipt of the doctorate to the time of the survey in 1966. Since the physicists were of widely varying ages in 1966, however, the length of the job histories also varied widely across individuals.

For this analysis, jobs were classified by three types of employers: (1) university departments whose "quality" was rated in Cartter's (1966) study; (2) four-year colleges and universities not rated by Cartter (usually lesser known institutions); and (3) nonacademic employers, including government and industry. These three employer types are the three states in a semi-Markov model of employer changes. The objective is to estimate the effects of several explanatory variables on transitions among these three states.

This situation departs somewhat from the typical semi-Markov model in that it is possible to make a transition from any of the three states back into the same state. Thus, one can make a transition from a nonacademic employer to another nonacademic employer. While this creates no analytical difficulties, it does increase the number of kinds of transition. With three origin states and three destination states, there are nine possible transitions, and a separate model will be estimated for each one of them.

The 477 physicists held a total of 1069 jobs during the period of observation. Of these jobs, 477 were censored because they were still in progress when the study was terminated. The remaining 592 jobs ended in transitions from one employer to another.

The explanatory variables were all treated as constant over time. They include a quality rating of each physicist's undergraduate institution, Cartter's (1966) rating of the doctoral department, number of years between the bachelors and doctoral degrees, a dummy variable indicating whether or not the individual received a postdoctoral fellowship, a dummy variable indicating U.S. citizenship, a dummy variable for "inbreeding" (employer is the physicist's doctoral department), number of previous jobs, Cartter rating of the current department (when available), career age (time since Ph.D.), and the calendar year in which the job began.

The model to be estimated is given by equation 20, where $a_{ij}(t - t')$ is left as an unspecified function of time. Hence, we have nine proportional hazards models, each of which can be estimated using the partial likelihood method. The first step is to divide the 1069 jobs into three groups by the three origin states. This yields 651 rated academic jobs, 212 unrated academic jobs, and 206 nonacademic jobs.

Beginning with the rated academic jobs, three models are estimated, one for each of the three destination states. For transitions to rated academic jobs, any such transition (there were 202) is treated as an event and all other outcomes are treated as censored. Similarly, in estimating the second model, any change to an unrated academic job is treated as an event and all other outcomes are treated as censored. The same procedure is used for the transitions from rated academic to nonacademic jobs. For all three models, the same subsample is analyzed and the same duration time is specified for each individual. The difference in the models is the specification of which duration times end in events and which are censored. Appendix B shows how this can easily be set up using the SAS program PHGLM.

Table 7 presents results from estimating these models. Examining the first three columns of Table 7, we see that most of the variables have estimated effects which are not significantly different from zero. For transitions from rated academic to rated academic, it appears that higher rates of transition are more characteristic of former postdoctoral fellows, those with more previous jobs, those whose jobs began in later calendar years, and those at younger career ages. Number of previous jobs and career age have particularly strong effects. Exponentiating the coefficient of .253 yields 1.29, which tells us that at each subsequent job the risk of a rated-academic to rated-academic transition increases by 29 percent. This is most likely a consequence of unexplained heterogeneity in the sample rather than a true causal effect of the number of jobs. Thus, we expect that those who have had many jobs in a given period of

TABLE 7
Estimates of Proportional Hazards Models for Transitions Among Three Types of Jobs

	1 From Rated Academic to:			2 From Unrated Academic to:			3 From Nonacademic to:		
Explanatory Variables	Rated Academic	Unrated Academic	Nonacademic	Rated Academic	Unrated Academic	Nonacademic	Rated Academic	Unrated Academic	Nonacademic
Undergraduate rating	.009	-.010	.013	.035	.014	.049	.003	.032	-.018
Graduate department rating	-.123	-.011	-.228	-.039	-.341	-.433	.121	-.269	.224
Time for Ph.D.	-.045	.037	-.017	-.106	.041	-.025	-.026	.157	-.106
Postdoctoral Fellow (D)[a]	.338*	-.009	.234	.467	.592	.415	-0.15	.157	-.058
U.S. Citizen (D)	-.138	-.340	-.191	-.222	-.370	.269	-.293	.153	-.468
Inbred (D)	.210	.538	.746*	-.749	-.484	.150	—	—	—
Number of previous jobs	.253***	.212	.284*	.338*	.146	.115	.237*	-.038	.248
Year job began	.021**	.025	.006	.041**	.002	.036	.045**	.001	-.014
Career age	-.204***	-.161***	-.163***	-.147***	-.123***	-.160***	-.089***	-.105*	-.075**
Cartter rating	.015	-.141	-.193	—	—	—	—	—	—
N of cases	651	651	651	212	212	212	206	206	206
N of job changes	202	42	48	55	43	20	109	25	48
-2 X log-likelihood	1934.97	426.54	486.57	436.52	336.24	148.97	960.77	218.82	413.41

a. (D) indicates dummy variable.
*Significant at .05 level.
**Significant at .01 level.
***Significant at .001 level.

time are more likely to change jobs again in the immediate future. The career age coefficient of $-.204$ exponentiates to $.82$, indicating that each additional year past the doctorate decreases the hazard of a transition by 18 percent; over a five-year period the hazard would be reduced by 64 percent. The latter figure is obtained by calculating $100 [1 - \exp(5 (-.204])]$. There are many possible explanations for this effect, but we shall not pursue them here.

Even fewer variables have significant effects in the next two columns representing transitions to unrated academic and nonacademic jobs. Although this is partly due to a decline in magnitude of some of the estimated effects, it is largely a consequence of the reduced number of observed transitions of these two types—there are only 42 changes from rated academic to unrated academic, and only 48 changes from rated academic to nonacademic. It is generally true in event history analysis that, while censored observations do contribute some information to the analysis, they do not add nearly as much information as uncensored observations. As a result, significance levels and standard errors will depend as much on the actual number of events as on the total number of observations.

The effect of career age is strong and roughly the same magnitude for all three types of transitions. The coefficient for number of previous jobs is also roughly the same magnitude for all three types, but its level of statistical significance varies greatly. The calendar year in which the job began has a significant effect only for rated to rated transitions, but its numerical magnitude is actually larger for rated to unrated moves. One surprising result is the substantial coefficient of "inbreeding" for rated academic to nonacademic transitions. When exponentiated, the coefficient of .746 becomes 2.11, indicating that physicists whose current job is in the university department in which they got their doctorate are more than twice as likely as others to move to a nonacademic job.

The next phase of the analysis is to examine the 212 jobs in unrated academic settings. Again the procedure is to estimate three models for this subsample. In each model, the event is a transition to a particular destination state and all other outcomes are treated as censored data. Cartter rating could not be included as an explanatory variable because, by definition of the origin state, it was not measured for these jobs. Results are shown in the three middle columns of Table 7. The overall picture is quite similar to that for transitions out of rated academic positions, except that even fewer variables have effects that are statistically significant. Again, this is partly due to the fact that both the overall number of cases and the number of observed transitions of each type are substantially reduced.

The final phase of the analysis is to repeat the process one more time for transitions out of nonacademic jobs. Both Cartter rating and "inbreeding" had to be omitted as explanatory variables because they were not meaningful for nonacademic jobs. Results in Table 7 are again quite similar to those for the other origin states.

What does this analysis tell us? The negative effect of career age is quite consistent across all the transition types. To a lesser degree, so are the effects of the number of previous jobs. The year the job began seems to be important in predicting transitions to rated academic jobs, but not to other destinations. The effects of postdoctoral fellowship and inbreeding show up for two types of transition but not for any others.

Simplifying the Model

Given the similarities across transition types, it is reasonable to inquire whether the results could be simplified in some way. In fact, there is no necessary reason why one should estimate separate models for all nine transition types. Both theory and empirical evidence can suggest combining either origin states or destination states or both. Table 8 gives results from estimating proportional hazards models in which the three destination states are combined while the distinction among origin states is maintained. The estimation procedure for these models was quite straightforward. As with the models in Table 7, intervals between events were subdivided by the three origin job types, and a separate model was estimated for each origin type. No distinction was made among destination states, however.

The coefficient estimates in Table 8 are approximately what one would expect just from averaging coefficients in Table 7. There is one notable change, however. For unrated academic jobs, the effect of a postdoctoral fellowship is statistically significant in Table 8 but not in Table 7. This is undoubtedly a consequence of the greater statistical power obtained by combining destination job types.

It is also possible to test whether the simplification obtained by combining destination job types is statistically justified. The null hypothesis is that the explanatory variables have identical coefficients across destination types but may differ by origin type. For each model estimated, both Tables 7 and 8 report the log-likelihood (multiplied by −2). A test statistic is obtained by adding all the log-likelihoods in Table

TABLE 8
Estimates of Proportional Hazards Models
Combining Destination Job Types

| Explanatory Variables | Origin Job Type | | |
	Rated Academic	Unrated Academic	Nonacademic
Undergraduate rating	.006	.030	.001
Graduate department rating	−.128	−.189	.081
Time for Ph.D.	−.028	−.017	−.017
Postdoctoral fellow (D)[a]	.271*	.492*	−.036
U. S. citizen (D)	−.175	−.181	−.274
Inbred (D)	.349*	−.494	−
Number of previous jobs	.247***	.234*	.213**
Year job began	.019**	.027**	.020*
Career age	−.188***	−.141***	−.086***
Career rating	−.044	−	−
N of cases	651	212	206
N of job changes	292	118	182
−2 X log-likelihood	2859.5	937.4	1614.8

a. (D) indicates dummy variable.
*Significant at .05 level.
**Significant at .01 level.
***Significant at .001 level.

7, doing the same in Table 8, and then taking the difference between the two sums. Thus, we have

$$48.8 = 5411.7 - 5362.9$$

Under the null hypothesis this statistic has a large-sample chi-square distribution with 54 degrees of freedom, which is the difference in the number of coefficients estimated in Table 7 and Table 8. Since this is far from significant, we may conclude that Table 8 is an acceptable simplification of Table 7.

An examination of the coefficients in Table 8 suggests that differences across origin job types are also small. To test whether further simplification is possible, a single model combining both origin job types and destination job types was estimated.[9] (Coefficient estimates are not shown.) For this model, the log-likelihood (multiplied by −2) was 6624.6. Taking the difference between this log-likelihood and the sum of the log-likelihoods in Table 8 yields a chi-square value of 1212.9 with only 17 degrees of freedom. Clearly, it is statistically unacceptable to collapse origin states.

One must also be aware that the approaches taken in this chapter, because they are based on observation of repeated events on each individual, suffer from an important limitation discussed in the last chapter. Specifically, it must be assumed that whatever dependence exists among the multiple intervals for a single individual is a consequence of the effects of the explanatory variables that are included in the model. Although the consequences of violating this assumption are not yet well understood, one can always take the conservative approach discussed in Chapter 6 of modifying the standard errors so that they reflect the number of individuals rather than the number of intervals or the number of transitions.

8. CONCLUSION

This monograph has focused on models in which the probability or hazard for the occurrence of events depends on one or more explanatory variables in a fashion that closely resembles multiple regression. Assuming that all relevant explanatory variables have been included, these models can usually be given a causal interpretation because the explanatory variables precede the event in time.[10]

Many biostatistical texts on survival analysis, especially those published before 1980, put considerable emphasis on "single-sample" methods, where the aim is to describe the distribution of event times, or on "two-sample" methods, where the aim is to compare two distributions of event times. The development of effective regression methods has rendered much of this material of limited value to social scientists, however. On one hand, the shape of the distribution can be very misleading unless one controls for sources of heterogeneity in the sample. On the other hand, statistical tests for comparing two distributions can be performed quite effectively within the regression framework by using a dummy explanatory variable.

Among the regression methods, the partial likelihood method with its associated models is clearly the most appealing approach. It can handle both continuous and discrete-time data with a single algorithm. It is much less restrictive than some of the more common parametric methods. Convenient and efficient programs are now widely available in standard statistical packages. And it can readily incorporate time-varying explanatory variables (although with greatly increased computational cost). For all these reasons, partial likelihood is a natural first choice in most situations.

There are two important limitations to the partial likelihood method, however. First, the dependence of the hazard on time is treated as a nuisance function that cancels out of the estimating equations. If the nature of this dependence is of interest in itself, it may be necessary to shift to a parametric model. Although some partial likelihood programs (e.g., BMDP2L) enable one to recover graphical estimates of the dependence on time, these are often inadequate to draw firm inferences.

The second limitation is that the proportional hazards model associated with the partial likelihood method does not include a disturbance term representing unobserved heterogeneity. In fact, Tuma (1982) has shown that partial likelihood will not accomodate any such disturbance term. When only unrepeated events are studied, it is not clear that this limitation is of any serious consequence. For repeated events, on the other hand, the inclusion of a disturbance term allows one to model dependence among repeated events for a single individual. Although the implications of such dependence have not been studied extensively, it would certainly be desirable to take it into account. Thus, those studying repeated events may want to consider some of the newer methods now being developed (Flinn and Heckman, 1982a, 1982b; Heckman and Singer, 1982).

One final note. The methods described in this monograph are practical, state-of-the-art approaches to the analysis of event histories. Nevertheless, one must keep in mind that event history analysis (by whatever name) is a rapidly expanding field to which a large number of people are contributing. It would be surprising indeed if many important new developments did not appear over the next several years. Since much of this literature is quite technical, the social scientist who wants to stay abreast of such developments may have to seek the advice of those who are actively involved in the field.

APPENDIX A:
MAXIMUM LIKELIHOOD AND PARTIAL LIKELIHOOD

This appendix is for those who have some acquaintance with maximum likelihood estimation and continuous distribution theory.

Maximum Likelihood

The principle of maximum likelihood is to choose as parameter estimates those values that maximize the likelihood (probability) of observing the data that have actually been observed. The first step in doing this is to express the likelihood of the data as a function of the unknown parameters. We shall see how this may be accomplished for parametric regression models.

Let us suppose that we have a sample of n independent individuals (i = 1, . . . ,n). For each individual, the data consist of (t_i, d_i, x_i) where t_i is either the time of event occurrence or the time of censoring, d_i is a dummy variable with a value of 1 if t_i is uncensored or 0 if t_i is censored, and x_i is a vector of explanatory variables. If observations are independent, the likelihood of the entire sample is just the product of the likelihoods for individual observations; that is,

$$L = \prod_{i=1}^{n} L_i \qquad [A1]$$

For uncensored observations, $L_i = f_i(t_i)$ where f_i is the probability density function (p.d.f.) for individual i. Note that f_i is subscripted to denote that the p.d.f. depends on the vector of explanatory variables, and thus differs across individuals. For censored data $L_i = 1 - F_i(t_i)$ where F_i is the cumulative distribution function (c.d.f.). Thus, $1 - F_i(t_i)$ is the probability that an event occurs *after* t_i for individual i. We can combine these formulas into

$$L = \prod_{i=1}^{n} (f_i(t_i))^{d_i}(1 - F_i(t_i))^{(1-d_i)} \qquad [A2]$$

To proceed further, we must make use of the following relationships between the hazard function, the p.d.f., and the c.d.f.:

$$h(t) = f(t)/(1 - F(t)) \tag{A3}$$

$$F(t) = 1 - \exp\left(-\int_0^t h(u)\,du\right) \tag{A4}$$

Equation A3 expresses the fact that the hazard is a conditional density, that is, it is the density for an event occurring at time t given that the event has not already occurred. Equation A4 is obtained by solving the first-order linear differential equation that arises from A3 (Kalbfleisch and Prentice, 1980: 6).

Substituting these two equations into the preceding equation gives an expression for the likelihood in terms of the hazard function:

$$L = \prod_{i=1}^{n} h_i(t_i)^{d_i} \exp\left(-\int_0^{t_i} h_i(u)\,du\right) \tag{A5}$$

Since maximizing the logarithm of a function is equivalent to maximizing the function itself, it is convenient to use the log-likelihood:

$$\log L = \sum_{i=1}^{n} d_i \log h_i(t_i) - \sum_{i=1}^{n} \int_0^{t_i} h_i(u)\,du \tag{A6}$$

At this point one can substitute for h_i whichever parametric model has been chosen. For example, in the case of the exponential regression model with a single explanatory variable, we have $h_i(t) = \exp(a + bx_i)$. This leads to

$$\log L = \sum_{i=1}^{n} d_i(a + bx_i) - \sum_{i=1}^{n} t_i \exp(a + bx_i) \tag{A7}$$

We have now succeeded in expressing the likelihood as a function of the unknown parameters, in this case a and b. The second step is to use some numerical method (usually iterative) to maximize log L with respect to a and b. The Newton-Raphson algorithm is usually satisfactory for this purpose, and has the advantage of producing standard errors of the estimates as a simple by-product. For further details, see Kalbfleisch and Prentice (1980) or Lawless (1982).

Partial Likelihood

Partial likelihood is like maximum likelihood in that the first step is to construct a likelihood function that depends on the unknown parameters and the observed data. The second step is to find parameter values that maximize this function. However, the usual likelihood function is a product of the likelihoods for all the *individuals* in the sample. The partial likelihood, on the other hand, is a product of likelihoods for all *events* that are observed to occur. Thus,

$$PL = \prod_{k=1}^{K} L_k \qquad \text{[A8]}$$

where PL is the partial likelihood and K is the total number of events in the sample.

To understand how the L_k's are constructed, let us consider the hypothetical example in Table A1. Here we have a sample of 10 cases, but only five events are observed; the other five cases are censored. Three of the observations are censored at time 12, presumably because the study ended at that point. Observation 4 is censored at time 5 and observation 6 is censored at time 9. In these two cases, censoring might have occurred because of death, deliberate withdrawal from the study, or inability to locate the individual in later follow-up interviews.

For convenience, the observations are arranged in order according to t_i, the time of censoring or event occurrence. The first event occurred to individual 1 at time 2. At that time, all 10 individuals in the sample were at risk of an event occurring. We now ask: Given that an event occurred at time 2, what is the probability that it occurred to individual 1 rather

TABLE A1
Example of Calculations for Partial Likelihood Estimation

i	t_i	k	L_k
1	2	1	$e^{bx_1} / (e^{bx_1} + e^{bx_2} + \ldots + e^{bx_{10}})$
2	4	2	$e^{bx_2} / (e^{bx_2} + e^{bx_3} + \ldots + e^{bx_{10}})$
3	5	3	$e^{bx_3} / (e^{bx_3} + e^{bx_4} + \ldots + e^{bx_{10}})$
4	5*		
5	6	4	$e^{bx_5} / (e^{bx_5} + e^{bx_6} + \ldots + e^{bx_{10}})$
6	9*		
7	11	5	$e^{bx_7} / (e^{bx_7} + e^{bx_8} + e^{bx_9} + e^{bx_{10}})$
8	12*		
9	12*		
10	12*		

NOTE: i = individuals; t_i = time of event occurrence or censoring for individual i; k = events.
*Censored.

than to one of the other 9 cases? This probability is L_1. It may be expressed as

$$L_1 = \frac{h_1(2)}{h_1(2) + h_2(2) + \ldots + h_{10}(2)} \quad [A9]$$

where, as before, $h_i(t)$ is the hazard for individual i at time t. Thus, we take the hazard at time 2 for the individual who experienced the event and divide by the sum of the hazards for all the individuals at risk at time 2. While A9 has considerable intuitive appeal, a formal derivation is actually quite tedious (Tuma, 1982) and will not be given here.

The expression for L_1 holds regardless of the model chosen for the dependence of the hazard on time and the explanatory variables. Under the proportional hazards model, however, it simplifies considerably. For that model

$$h_i(t) = \exp(a(t) + bx_i) = \exp(a(t)) \exp(bx_i) \quad [A10]$$

where x_i is a column vector of explanatory variables for individual i, and b is a row vector of coefficients. When this is substituted into the expression for L_1, the quantity $exp(a(t))$ cancels from each term, leaving

$$L_1 = \frac{exp(bx_1)}{exp(bx_1) + exp(bx_2) + \ldots + exp(bx_{10})} \qquad [A11]$$

It is this cancellation that makes it possible to estimate the coefficient vector b while completely disregarding the unspecified function a(t).

L_2 is constructed in the same way. Given that an event occurred at time 4, L_2 is the probability that the event occurred to individual 2 rather than to one of the other individuals at risk at time 4. The only difference is that individual 1, having already experienced an event, is no longer at risk at time 4. Therefore,

$$L_2 = \frac{exp(bx_2)}{exp(bx_2) + exp(bx_3) + \ldots + exp(bx_{10})} \qquad [A12]$$

Formulas for L_3, L_4 and L_5 are given in Table A1.

Note that the value of each L_k does not depend on the exact time at which the kth event occurs. It could occur at any point after the $(k - 1)^{th}$ event and before the $(k + 1)^{th}$ event and still have the same magnitude. It is only the order of the events that affects the partial likelihood.

Once the partial likelihood is constructed, it can be maximized like an ordinary likelihood function using the Newton-Raphson algorithm (Kalbfleisch and Prentice, 1980; Lawless, 1982).

APPENDIX B:
PROGRAM LISTINGS FOR GLIM, SAS, AND BMDP EXAMPLES

[A] *Estimation of exponential regression model using GLIM3* (see Chapter 3).

(1) $UNITS 432

(2) $DATA ARST WEEK FIN AGE RACE WEXP MAR PARO PRIO AGE1 EDUC WORK

(3) $DINPUT 1

(4) $CALC LWK = %LOG(WEEK)

(5) $YVAR ARST

(6) $ERROR P

(7) $LINK L

(8) $OFFSET LWK

(9) $FIT FIN, AGE, RACE, WEXP, MAR, PARO, PRIO, AGE1, EDUC, WORK

(10) $DISPLAY E

TRANSLATION

(1) Set sample size at 432.

(2) Name the variables in the order in which they will be read. ARST is a dummy variable with a value of 1 if the person was arrested during the 12-month follow-up, otherwise 0. It is the censoring indicator. WEEK is the number of weeks from release to first arrest, set equal to 52 for those not arrested.

(3) Input the data from logical unit 1 in free format.

(4) Define LWK to be the natural logarithm of WEEK.

(5) Declare ARST to be the dependent variable.

(6) Specify a Poisson error distribution.

(7) Specify a logarithmic link, that is, the logarithm of the conditional mean of the dependent variable is a linear function of the explanatory variables.

(8) Include LWK as an explanatory variable, but force its coefficient to be 1.

(9) Estimate a model with the 10 named explanatory variables.

(10) Display the coefficients and standard errors.

The rationale for the peculiar model specified in lines 5-8 is given in Aitkin and Clayton (1980). If there are no censored data, the model can be fit more directly by specifying WEEK as the dependent variable, a logarithmic link, and an exponential error distribution.

[B] *Partial likelihood estimation using SAS procedure PHGLM* (see Chapter 4).

(1) PROC SORT DATA = LIFE.DATA;

(2) BY DESCENDING WEEK;

(3) PROC PHGLM;

(4) EVENT ARST;

(5) MODEL WEEK = FIN AGE RACE WEXP MAR PARO PRIO AGE1 EDUC WORK;

TRANSLATION

(1), (2)   Sort the data by week of arrest (or last week observed), in descending order. PHGLM requires that data first be sorted by the time of the event or censoring.

(3)   Invoke PHGLM.

(4)   Declare ARST as the censoring indicator (1 if arrested, 0 if not).

(5)   Estimate a model with WEEK as the event time and the 10 named explanatory variables.

[C] *Partial likelihood with a time-varying explanatory variable using BMDP2L* (see Chapter 4).

(1)   /INPUT UNIT = 3. CODE = BMPLIFE.

(2)   /FORM TIME = WEEK. STATUS = ARST. RESPONSE = 1.

(3) /REGRESSION
    COVARIATE = FIN,AGE,RACE,WEXP,MAR,PARO,
    PRIO,AGE1,EDUC.

(4) ADD = WRK.

(5) AUXILIARY = WORK1 TO WORK52.

FORTRAN subroutine, which must be compiled and linked with main program:

(6) SUBROUTINE P2LFUN (Z,ZT,AUX,TIME,NFXCOV,
    NADD,NAUX,ISUB,X)

(7) DIMENSION Z(9),ZT(1),AUX(52)

(8) ZT(1) = AUX(TIME)

(9) RETURN

(10) END

TRANSLATION

(1) Read a BMDP file called BMPLIFE from unit 3.

(2) Declare WEEK as the event time, ARST as the censoring indicator, and 1 as the value of ARST indicating uncensored data.

(3) Specify a model with the nine named time-constant explanatory variables.

(4) Include a time-varying explanatory variable named WRK, not yet defined.

(5) Declare 52 variables to be used in defining the values of WRK. These are 52 dummy variables with a value of 1 if the person was employed in a particular week, otherwise 0.

(6) Subroutine statement described in BMDP manual. Note inclusion of last variable X, which is not documented in 1981 manual. This is a missing value indicator, not used in this example.

(7) Construct arrays of nine constant explanatory variables, one time-varying explanatory variable, and 52 auxiliary variables.

(8) Define WRK at a particular TIME to have the value of the auxiliary variable measured at that TIME. Here TIME is equivalent to the variable WEEK.

(9) Return to the main program.

[D] *Partial likelihood for nine types of transition using SAS PHGLM* (see Chapter 8).

```
(1)   DATA PHYS.JOB;
(2)   SET PHYS.JOB;
(3)   IF TYPE2 = 1 THEN EV1 = 1; ELSE EV1 = 0;
(4)   IF TYPE2 = 2 THEN EV2 = 1; ELSE EV2 = 0;
(5)   IF TYPE2 = 3 THEN EV3 = 1; ELSE EV3 = 0;
(6)   PROC SORT;
(7)   BY DESCENDING DUR1;
(8)   DATA;
(9)   SET PHYS.JOB;
(10)  IF TYPE1 NE 1 THEN DELETE;
(11)  PROC PHGLM;
(12)  EVENT EV1;
(13)  MODEL DUR1 = UND GRAD TIME PDOC US INBR
      NJOBS YEAR CAGE CARTT;
(14)  PROC PHGLM;
(15)  EVENT EV2;
(16)  MODEL DUR1 = UND GRAD TIME PDOC US INBR
      NJOBS YEAR CAGE CARTT;
(17)  PROC PHGLM;
(18)  EVENT EV3;
(19)  MODEL DUR1 = UND GRAD TIME PDOC US INBR
      NJOBS YEAR CAGE CARTT;
(20)  DATA;
(21)  SET PHYS.JOB;
(22)  IF TYPE1 NE 2 THEN DELETE;
```

76

(23) PROC PHGLM;

(24) EVENT EV1;

(25) MODEL DUR1 = UND GRAD TIME PDOC US INBR
NJOBS YEAR CAGE;

(26) PROC PHGLM;

(27) EVENT EV2;

(28) MODEL DUR1 = UND GRAD TIME PDOC US INBR
NJOBS YEAR CAGE;

(29) PROC PHGLM;

(30) EVENT EV3;

(31) MODEL DUR1 = UND GRAD TIME PDOC US INBR
NJOBS YEAR CAGE;

(32) DATA;

(33) SET PHYS.JOB;

(34) IF TYPE1 NE 3 THEN DELETE;

(35) PROC PHGLM;

(36) EVENT EV1;

(37) MODEL DUR1 = UND GRAD TIME PDOC US NJOBS
YEAR CAGE;

(38) PROC PHGLM;

(39) EVENT EV2;

(40) MODEL DUR1 = UND GRAD TIME PDOC US NJOBS
YEAR CAGE;

(41) PROC PHGLM;

(42) EVENT EV3;

(43) MODEL DUR1 = UND GRAD TIME PDOC US NJOBS
YEAR CAGE;

TRANSLATION

(1-5) Create dummy variables corresponding to the three types
of destination.

(6-7) Sort the data by duration of job.

(8-10)   Exclude all origin jobs other than rated academic.
(11-13) Fit a model for destinations to rated academic jobs.
(14-16) Fit a model for destinations to unrated academic jobs.
(17-19) Fit a model for destinations to nonacademic jobs.
(20-22) Exclude all origin jobs other than unrated academic.
(23-31) Fit models for the three types of destination.
(32-34) Exclude all origin jobs other than nonacademic.
(36-43) Fit models for the three types of destination.

APPENDIX C:
COMPUTER PROGRAMS

Here is a brief description of several publicly available computer programs that will estimate one or more of the models discussed above. It is current as of spring 1984. Table C1 gives a summary of the models that can be estimated and some of the features that are available.

BMDP2L

BMDP2L (Dixon, 1981) is a program in the BMDP statistical package for estimating proportional hazards models. It has many useful features and options. For further information, contact

BMDP Statistical Software
1964 Westwood Blvd., Suite 202
Los Angeles, CA 90025
(213) 475-5700

CENSOR

CENSOR (Meeker and Duke, 1981) is a FORTRAN program for estimating parametric models. Although it was designed primarily for fitting various distributions to univariate data, it will also estimate several regression models. It is currently available from the author for $50. Contact

William Q. Meeker, Jr.
Department of Statistics
Iowa State University
Ames, IA 50001
(515) 294-5336

GLIM

GLIM (Baker and Nelder, 1978) is a FORTRAN program for interactive fitting of "generalized linear models," a family that includes ordinary regression, logit, probit, and log-linear models. If there are no censored data, GLIM3 can fit the exponential regression model directly. Using special procedures (Aitkin and Clayton, 1980; Roger and Peacock, 1983), it can also fit the exponential, Weibull, and log-logistic models to censored data. GLIM4, which was scheduled for release in the summer of 1984, is supposed to fit these models directly, as well as the proportional hazards model. Contact

The GLIM Co-ordinator
NAG Central Office
Mayfield House
256 Banbury Road
Oxford 0X2 7DE
UK

PHGLM

PHGLM (SAS Institute, 1983) is part of the supplemental program library of the SAS statistical package. It does partial likelihood estimation of the proportional hazards model. Because it is user contributed, it is not fully supported by SAS. PHGLM is one of the easiest partial likelihood programs to use, but does not have as many features as BMDP2L or SURVREG. Contact

SAS Institute Inc.
Box 8000
Cary, NC 27511

RATE

RATE (Tuma, 1979) is a FORTRAN program to estimate the Markov renewal model of Chapter 7, and several variants of that model. Version 3, recently released, is priced at approximately $175 and is available from

DMA Corporation
P.O. Box 881
Palo Alto, CA 94302
(415) 856-4770

SURVREG

SURVREG (Preston and Clarkson, 1983) is a FORTRAN program for estimating both parametric and proportional hazards models. It

80

TABLE C1
Models and Features Available in Six Computer Programs

	BMDP2L	CENSOR	GLIM3	PHGLM[a]	RATE[b]	SURVREG
Model						
Proportional hazards	X			X	X	X
Weibull		X	X			X
Gompertz					X	
Exponential		X	X		X	X
Log-normal		X				X
Log-logistic		X	X			X
Feature						
Stratification	X			X		X
Time-varying explanatory variable	X				_c	X
Diagnostic plots	X	X	X	X		X

a. 1983 version.
b. Version 2.
c. Allows time-varying explanatory variables for parametric models, but not for proportional hazards model.

appears to be one of the most general and flexible programs available. Designed for interactive use, it can also be used in batch mode. It is currently available for $100 from the author:

Douglas B. Clarkson
Department of Mathematics
University of Missouri
St. Louis, MO 63121

NOTES

1. In some cases, it may be more appropriate to use lagged values of the explanatory variables. See Chapter 3 for more details. In other cases, the explanatory variables may be measured more frequently or less frequently than the intervals used for constructing the discrete-time observations. Allison (1982) and Tuma (1982) discuss different ways of dealing with this problem.

2. It is also possible to estimate models in which the coefficients of one or more explanatory variables are allowed to vary at each of the discrete time points. This is accomplished by multiplying a given explanatory variable by each of the four dummy variables used in Model 2. These product terms are then added to Model 2 to create an expanded model.

3. In fairness, it should be noted that these results are very similar to the results obtained by Rossi, Berk, and Lenihan (1980) using the much more familiar procedure of ordinary least squares with a dummy dependent variable indicating whether or not an arrest occurred. As noted in Chapter 1, their procedure discards information on variability in the timing of arrest for those who were arrested. That doesn't seem to make much difference in this case, however, perhaps because only 27 percent of the cases were arrested, or because the interval of observation was relatively short.

4. In some cases, there will be sufficient evidence to discriminate among alternative functional forms. In demography, for example, it is well known that the Gompertz distribution provides a better description of human mortality at ages above 25 than does the Weibull distribution.

5. For this reason, it is possible to use the partial likelihood method to estimate regression models for ordinal data other than event history data. This approach is closely related to the regression methods for ordinal data proposed by McCullagh (1980).

6. This can be explained as follows. Suppose we wish to estimate the model

$$\log h(t) = a(t) + b_1 x + b_2 w(t)$$

where t is the length of time since a marriage began, $h(t)$ is the hazard for divorce at time t, $w(t)$ is the wife's age at time t, x is some explanatory variable that is constant over time, and $a(t)$ is an arbitrary function. Notice that $w(t) = t + w(0)$ where $w(0)$ is the wife's age at marriage. Substituting into the model above gives

$$\log h(t) = a(t) + b_2 t + b_1 x + b_2 w(0)$$

This may be written as

$$\log h(t) = a_2(t) + b_1 x + b_2 w(0)$$

where $a_2(t) = a(t) + b_2 t$, a different arbitrary function of time. Thus, the time-varying component of the wife's age is absorbed into the arbitrary function.

81

7. Most programs for partial likelihood estimation presume that all individuals enter the risk set at the same time, t = 0. What is needed is a program that will allow individuals to enter the risk set at different points on the time axis.

8. Right censoring means that the length of an interval is known to be *greater* than a certain value, but the exact length is not known. Left censoring, on the other hand, means that the length of an interval is known to be *less* than some value even though the exact length is not known (Turnbull, 1974). By these definitions, the initial intervals for the kind of data under discussion are right censored rather than left censored. These intervals cannot be treated by the usual methods for right-censored data, however, because initial intervals have a different distribution than later intervals (Flinn and Heckman, 1982a, 1982b).

9. A complication in estimating this model is that some of the variables were not defined for some of the origin states. In the combined model, the "extra" variables were assigned values of 0 whenever they were not defined for a particular origin job type.

10. Note, however, that the time-ordering may be somewhat ambiguous in the case of time-varying explanatory variables. In many cases, individuals are able to anticipate the occurrence of an event and alter their behavior prior to the actual occurrence. An obvious example is the case in which women who are expecting a child drop out of school prior to the actual birth.

REFERENCES

AITKIN, M. and CLAYTON, D. (1980) "The fitting of exponential, Weibull, 'and extreme value distributions to complex censored survival data using GLIM." Applied Statistics 29: 156-163.

ALLISON, P. D. (1982) "Discrete-time methods for the analysis of event histories," pp. 61-98 in S. Leinhardt (ed.) Sociological Methodology 1982. San Francisco: Jossey-Bass.

BAKER, R. J. and J. A. NELDER (1978) The GLIM System. Oxford: Numerical Algorithms Group.

BRESLOW, N. E. (1974) "Covariance analysis of censored survival data." Biometrics 30: 89-99.

BROWN, C. C. (1975) "On the use of indicator variables for studying the time-dependence of parameters in a response time model." Biometrics 31: 863-872.

CARTTER, ALLAN M. (1966) An Assessment of Quality in Graduate Education. Washington, DC: American Council on Education.

Cattel Press (1966) American Men and Women of Science. New York: Bowker.

COLEMAN, J. S. (1981) Longitudinal Data Analysis. New York: Basic Books.

COX, D. R. (1972) "Regression models and life tables." Journal of the Royal Statistical Society, Series B 34: 187-202.

CROWLEY, J. and B. E. STORER (1983) "Comment on 'A reanalysis of the Stanford heart transplant data.'" Journal of the American Statistical Association 78: 277-281.

DIPRETE, T. A. (1981) "Unemployment over the life cycle: racial differences and the effect of changing economic conditions." American Journal of Sociology 87: 286-307.

DIXON, W. J. (1981) BMDP Statistical Software. Berkeley: University of California Press.

EFRON, B. (1977) "The efficiency of Cox's likelihood function for censored data." Journal of the American Statistical Association 72: 557-565.

ELANDT-JOHNSON, R. C. and N. L. JOHNSON (1980) Survival Models and Data Analysis. New York: John Wiley.

FAREWELL, V. T. and R. L. PRENTICE (1980) "The approximation of partial likelihood with emphasis on case-control studies." Biometrika 67: 273-278.

FLINN, C. J. and J. J. HECKMAN (1982a) "New methods for analyzing individual event histories," pp. 99-140 in S. Leinhardt (ed.) Sociological Methodology 1982. San Francisco: Jossey-Bass.

——— (1982b) "Models for the analysis of labor force dynamics," pp. 35-95 in G. Rhodes and R. Basmann (eds.) Advances in Econometrics. New Haven, CT: JAI.

GAIL, M. H., T. J. SANTNER, and C. C. BROWN (1980) "An analysis of comparative carcinogenesis experiments based on multiple times to tumor." Biometrics 36: 255-266.

GLASSER, M. (1967) "Exponential survival with covariance." Journal of the American Statistical Association 62: 561-568.

GOODMAN, L. A. (1975) "The relationship between modified and usual multiple regression approaches to the analysis of dichotomous variables," in D. R. Heise (ed.), Sociological Methodology 1976. San Francisco: Jossey-Bass.

GROSS, A. J. and V. A. CLARK (1975) Survival Distributions: Reliability Applications in the Biomedical Sciences. New York: John Wiley.

84

HAGSTROM, W. O. (1974) "Competition in science." American Sociological Review 39: 1-18.

HANUSHEK, E. A. and J. E. Jackson (1977) Statistical Methods for Social Scientists. New York: Academic.

HARRELL, F. (1980) "The PHGLM procedure," pp. 119-131 in SAS Supplemental Library User's Guide. Cary, NC: SAS Institute Inc.

HECKMAN, J. J. and B. SINGER (1982) "The identification problem in econometric models for duration data," in W. Hildebrand (ed.) Advances in Econometrics. Cambridge: Cambridge University Press.

HOLFORD, T. R. (1980) "The analysis of rates and of survivorship using log-linear models." Biometrics 36: 299-305.

HOLT, J. D. (1978) "Competing risk analysis with special reference to matched pair experiments." Biometrika 65: 159-165.

KALBFLEISCH, J. D. and R. L. PRENTICE (1980) The Statistical Analysis of Failure Time Data. New York: John Wiley.

KAY, R. (1977) "Proportional hazard regression models and the analysis of censored survival data." Applied Statistics 26: 227-237.

KNOKE, D. (1982) "The spread of municipal reform: temporal, spatial and social dynamics." American Journal of Sociology 87: 1314-1339.

LAIRD, N. and D. OLIVIER (1981) "Covariance analysis of censored survival data using log-linear analysis techniques." Journal of the American Statistical Association 76: 231-240.

LAWLESS, J. F. (1982) Statistical Models and Methods for Lifetime Data. New York: John Wiley.

LONG, J. S., P. D. ALLISON, and R. McGINNIS (1979) "Entrance into the academic career." American Sociological Review 44: 816-830.

MANTEL, N. and B. HANKEY (1978) "A logistic regression analysis of response-time data where the hazard function is time-dependent." Communications in Statistics—Theory and Methods A7: 333-347.

McCULLAGH, P. (1980) "Regression models for ordinal data." Journal of the Royal Statistical Society, Series B 42: 109-142.

McGINNIS, R. (1968) "A stochastic model of social mobility." American Sociological Review 33: 363-390.

MEEKER, W. Q. and S. D. DUKE (1981) "CENSOR—a user-oriented computer program for life data analysis." American Statistician 35: 112.

NELSON, W. (1982) Applied Life Data Analysis. New York: John Wiley.

PETERSON, A. V., Jr. (1976) "Bounds for a joint distribution with fixed sub-distribution functions: application to competing risks." Proceedings of the National Academy of Sciences 73: 11-13.

POLLARD, A. H., F. YUSUF, and G. N. POLLARD (1981) Demographic Techniques. Sydney: Pergamon.

PRENTICE, R. L. and L. A. GLOECKLER (1978) "Regression analysis of grouped survival data with application to breast cancer." Biometrics 34: 57-67.

PRENTICE, R. L., B. J. WILLIAMS and A. V. PETERSON (1981) "On the regression analysis of multivariate failure data." Biometrika 68: 373-374.

PRESTON, D. L. and D. B. CLARKSON (1983) "SURVREG: a program for the interactive analysis of survival regression models." American Statistician 37: 174.

ROGER, J. H. and S. D. PEACOCK (1983) "Fitting the scale as a GLIM parameter for Weibull, extreme value, logistic, and log-logistic regression models with censored data." GLIM Newsletter 6: 30-37.

ROOSE, K. D. and C. J. ANDERSEN (1970) A Rating of Graduate Programs. Washington, DC: American Council on Education.

ROSSI, P. H., R. A. BERK, and K. J. LENIHAN (1980) Money, Work and Crime: Some Experimental Results. New York: Academic.

SAS Institute Inc. (1983) SAS Supplemental Library User's Guide. Cary, NC: SAS Institute Inc.

SINGER, B. and S. SPILERMAN (1976) "The representation of social processes by Markov models." American Journal of Sociology 82: 1-54.

SCHOENFELD, D. (1982) "Partial residuals for the proportional hazards regression model." Biometrika 69: 239-241.

SØRENSEN, A. B. (1977) "Estimating rates from retrospective questions," pp. 209-223 in D. R. Heise (ed.) Sociological Methodology 1977. San Francisco: Jossey-Bass.

SPSS Inc. (1983) SPSS User's Guide. New York: McGraw-Hill.

THOMPSON, W. A., Jr. (1977) "On the treatment of grouped observations in life studies." Biometrics 33: 463-470.

TSIATIS, A. (1975) "A nonidentifiability aspect of the problem of competing risks." Proceedings of the National Academy of Sciences 72: 20-22.

TUMA, N. B. (1982) "Nonparametric and partially parametric approaches to event history analysis," pp. 1-60 in S. Leinhardt (ed.) Sociological Methodology 1982. San Francisco: Jossey-Bass.

——— (1979) "Invoking RATE." Program manual. (unpublished)

——— (1978) "Effects of labor market structure on job-shift patterns." Presented at the 73rd Annual Meeting of the American Sociological Association, San Francisco.

——— (1976) "Rewards, resources and the rate of mobility: a nonstationary multivariate stochastic model." American Sociological Review 41: 338-360.

——— and M. T. HANNAN (1978) "Approaches to the censoring problem in analysis of event histories," in K. F. Schuessler (ed.) Sociological Methodology 1979. San Francisco: Jossey-Bass.

——— and L. D. GROENEVELD (1979) "Dynamic analysis of event histories." American Journal of Sociology 84: 820-854.

TURNBULL, B. W. (1974) "Nonparametric estimation of a survivorship function with doubly censored data." Journal of the American Statistical Association 69: 74-80.

ZIPPIN, C. and P. ARMITAGE (1966) "Use of concomitant variables and incomplete survival information in the estimation of an exponential survival parameter." Biometrics 22: 665-672.

PAUL D. ALLISON is Associate Professor of Sociology at the University of Pennsylvania, where he teaches quantitative methods. Event history analysis is currently his major research interest, but he has also published papers on log-linear and logit analysis, Markov processes, measures of inequality, and missing data. Approximately half his published work has been on the sociology of scientific careers.

Quantitative Applications in the Social Sciences

(a Sage University Papers Series)

$5.00 each

SAGE PUBLICATIONS, INC.
P.O. BOX 5024
BEVERLY HILLS, CALIFORNIA 90210

Place
Stamp
here